GREAT

AMERICAN

QUILTS

1987

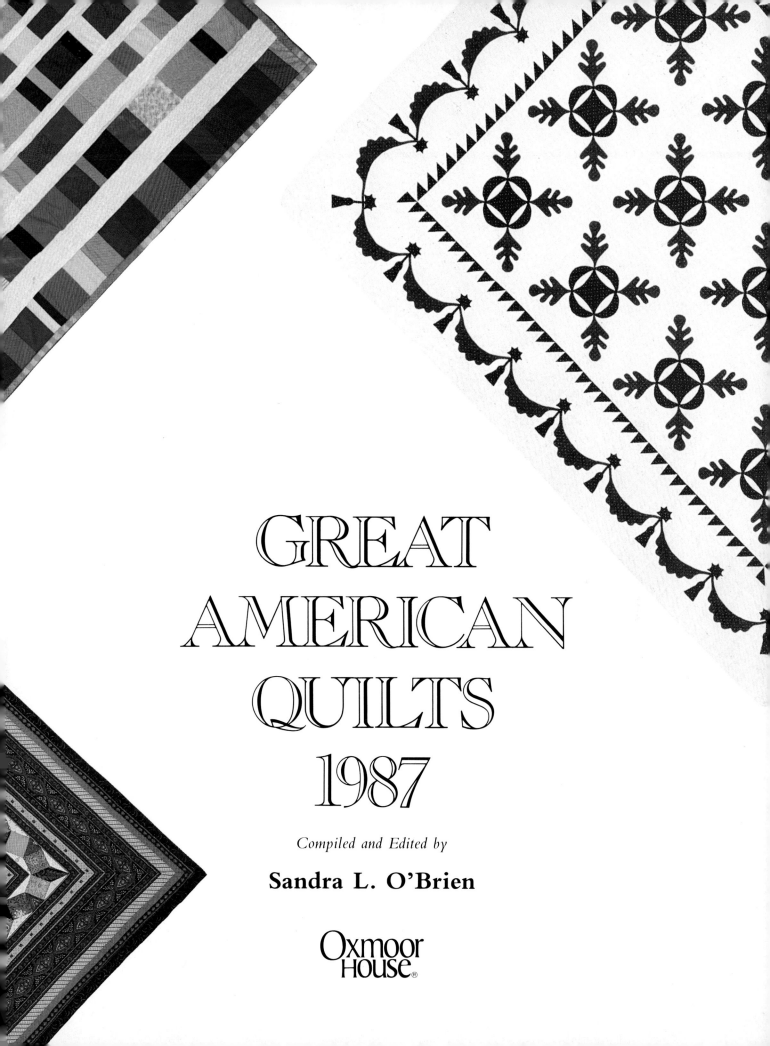

GREAT AMERICAN QUILTS 1987

Compiled and Edited by

Sandra L. O'Brien

Oxmoor
House.

Library of Congress Catalog Number: 86-62283
ISBN: 0-8487-0696-X
ISSN: 0890-8222
Manufactured in the United States of America
First Printing 1987

Executive Editor: Candace N. Conard
Production Manager: Jerry Higdon
Associate Production Manager: Rick Litton
Art Director: Bob Nance

Great American Quilts 1987

Editorial Assistant: Margaret Allen Northen
Copy Chief: Mary Jean Haddin
Designer: Earl Freedle
Artist: Larry Hunter
Photographers: Gary Clark, Mary-Gray Hunter,
 Cheryl Sales, Sylvia Martin, Jim Bathie, Beth Maynor,
 Courtland Richards

CONTENTS

EDITOR'S NOTE

Compiling a book is much like developing the patchwork design for a quilt. You have the certainties: what you want it to look like and why you want to do it. But there are also the variables, or the uncertainties: Will it work? Will it look good? And will others like it?

When the editors of Oxmoor House went seeking America's quilters, our idea was that quilters throughout the United States want to know what their neighboring quilters are doing. We believed quilters were curious about other quilters—what kind of wonderful quilts they were creating, how they developed their designs, where they quilted, how long they had been quilting, and what the story was behind their quilts. But would quilters want to share their ideas and patterns in print for all the country to see, and would they lend us their quilts for six or more months while we examined, measured, and photographed?

As we reviewed the first submissions, our uncertainties changed to certainties. Yes, quilters want to share. Yes, they want to be published. And yes, they will even give up their quilts for a couple of months. So Oxmoor House *was* going to publish a book, because the quilters of America told us that they wanted one and, most of all, because they said they wanted to be a part of it.

Now the task was at hand to select quilters for our first book. Through daily afternoon sessions of four to five hours, we meticulously reviewed slides, prints, and submission forms. Every word was read and re-read. All of you devoted countless unselfish hours to completing our forms, so it was only reasonable for us to do the same for you.

It quickly became evident to us that quilting is ingrained in your life-style. As Zoe Krcelic of Columbus, Mississippi, told us, "The only room not stacked with quilting supplies is the bathroom!" Another quilter, Sandra Wells of Clayton, Indiana, confessed, "It's something I can't stay away from, no matter what else I should be doing." And Margaret Rogers of Porterville, California, commented, "The floor hoop sits wherever I am."

Others of you remarked on the sense of accomplishment quilting gives you. Gail MacPhee of Central Falls, Rhode Island, summarized many quilters' feelings when she said, "It just makes me feel so good, being wrapped up in something I made from scraps of material." Or as Sherry A. Paris of Quincy, Indiana, put it, "I love the part most when I throw the quilt across my bed for all the world to see!"

Along with your dedication to quilting, a deep sense of responsibility to your families is apparent in your letters, too. There is a steadfast allegiance to quilting in dens or family rooms so that family members are not deprived of your presence. Willing husbands are included on numerous trips to fabric shops and quilt shows, and no family fishing trip is complete without those layers of fabric suspended between the rings of a quilting hoop.

We thoroughly enjoyed getting to know you through your letters and notes, and we hope you, too, will enjoy getting to know the quilters we selected for 1987 in our *Quilts Across America* chapter. Along with a brief biographical sketch, you will find one or more of their quilts, the story behind them, and complete directions with diagrams, if necessary, and full-size patterns.

Besides quilts from individuals, submissions were welcomed from guilds. Our *Bee Quilters* chapter concentrates on guilds—their quilts, their activities, and some interesting highlights on the mechanics of group quilting.

As the selections were being made, the quilts submitted were falling into additional categories. There were numerous stories about family traditions in quilting, too good to pass by. A chapter just on *Traditions in Quilting* was the answer, featuring individuals, their stories, and how the quilting tradition has affected their lives.

Then there was a group of quilters who used new techniques, or introduced techniques from non-quilting areas into quilting, or manipulated traditional patterns for new visual effects. This became our chapter featuring quilters who used similar, and yet unique, quiltmaking techniques or design mechanics. This year, *Log Cabin Turnaround* focuses on the Log Cabin block and the multitude of things quilters have done with it. Next year, the chapter will spotlight a different aspect of quilting.

Many elegant quilts deserved recognition, but detailed designs with intricate and complex piecing made duplication of patterns, for our purposes, too difficult; and yet, these quilts were too magnificent to leave out. Thus *Designer Gallery* was born. In the gallery quilters can view and appreciate these one-of-a-kind and/or very elaborate quilts, and get to know the skilled craftspeople behind them. For an instant dose of inspiration, spend some time in the gallery.

Quilters, this is your book. The thoughts and statements are yours. Quilting talent abounds throughout America. Discipline and dedication and love were personified in every quilt reviewed. We thank you for sharing a piece of your heart with us and all quilters.

Preliminary Instructions

All pattern pieces include ¼″ seam allowance. Some oversize pieces are placed on a grid, with scale information noted.

Fabric requirements are based on 44″-45″-wide fabric with trimmed selvages. Generous fabric allowance is made for all fabric requirements. Fabric requirements are given for one-piece borders, and continuous bias strips.

Prepare fabrics before marking and cutting by washing, drying, and pressing.

LOG CABIN TURNAROUND

Separated from European traditions and fashions, America's pioneers chose values that dictated a style of necessity—an efficient, streamlined style, free of frills and extravagance. Most historians say it was a lack of skill and supplies that encouraged this spare style. But perhaps it was also a subconscious effort made by colonists who had labored on the palaces of Europe, or witnessed the excesses of the ruling classes. Perhaps they chose to leave such excesses behind and begin anew in America.

With needle and thread the pioneer woman recorded the birth of American behavior and style, especially in her quilting. Nowhere is this more evident than with the Log Cabin block pattern. Though the pattern dates back to ancient Egyptian times, the interest of the pioneer quiltmaker was in capturing the life around her in fabric stories. Whether her pencil-thin scraps of fabric reminded her of logs, or whether the layers of logs that encircled her world influenced her fabric cutting is not known. What *is* known is that her thoughts centered around home, and so did her piecework.

Within a short time the Log Cabin center square became symbolic of the heart of the home: its hearth, its chimney, or its lantern. Each successive fabric strip represented the cabin logs, symbolic of layers of love stacked around the steadfast center. Using her imagination and ingenuity, the quilter arranged and rearranged Log Cabin blocks to imitate the sights around her. Painstakingly, hands sequenced Log Cabin blocks to document life close to nature, as evidenced by Barn Raising, Straight Furrows, and Streak o' Lightning.

Similarly, quiltmakers today are painstakingly arranging Log Cabin blocks to reflect the life around them. Log Cabin blocks are being turned and reversed, expanded and narrowed, trimmed and extended until sometimes the block itself seems to disappear. But true to its legend, the Log Cabin block is steadfast, a survivor; it will not vanish. It continues to embody the characteristics that made it so popular: ease of assembly, pleasant geometric interaction, and alluring simplicity that can be forged into complex structures.

Log Cabin Basics

Log Cabin blocks can be assembled with or without a template pattern. Instructions are given below for basic machine piecing of Log Cabin blocks without templates. Since the mechanics for assembling a Log Cabin block are essentially the same, each set of instructions for quilts in this chapter gives only Log Cabin square and strip measurements. If you have never made a Log Cabin block, follow the instructions below and make one for practice.

Log Cabin Block Assembly

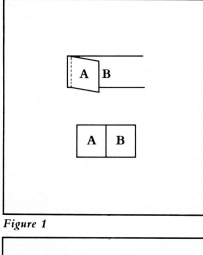

Figure 1

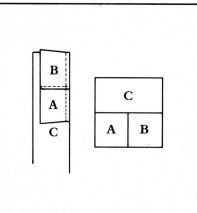

Figure 2

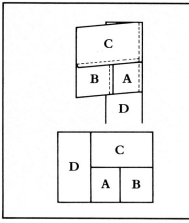

Figure 3

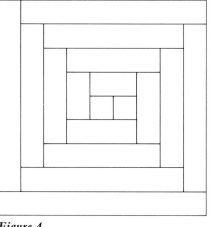

Figure 4

Instructions are given for the traditional spiraling Log Cabin block. They are adaptable for piecing of other Log Cabin Blocks such as Courthouse Steps, Off-Center, and other variations. All pieces are joined with ¼″ seam allowance.

1. Cut a 1½″ square (A) for the center. Note: The size of the center square and the log strips will vary with the type of Log Cabin block you are making. Join the square to a 1½″-wide strip (B) of fabric. Trim the strip (B) even with the square (A). (Figure 1.)

2. Lay joined squares (A, B) across a 1½″ strip (C) of fabric and sew. (Figure 2.) Trim strip (C) even with squares A and B.

3. Rotate joined pieces, sew to 1½″-wide strip (D) as shown (Figure 3), and trim strip (D).

4. Continue adding strips in this fashion, until desired Log Cabin block size is reached. Notice that the last strip sewn in place is the first one to be joined to the next strip. If you decide to join 4 levels of 1½″ log strips to your 1½″ center square, finished size of your Log Cabin block should be 9″ square. (Figure 4.)

Types of Log Cabin Blocks

Illustrated here are some of the most common Log Cabin block variations.

The traditional spiraling block changes its character by the alternation of color tones.

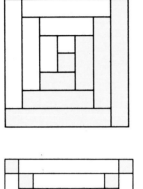 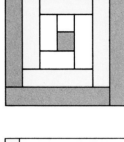 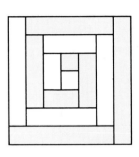

The Chimney and Cornerstone blocks repeat the center square throughout the block, often seen as a large X across the block.

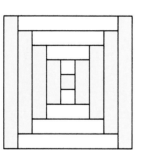 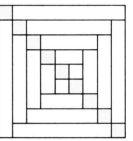 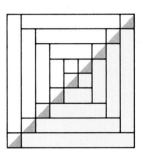

The Courthouse Steps is assembled by joining log strips of equal width to each side of the center square. Varied square and strip dimensions as well as color placement alter the block's appearance.

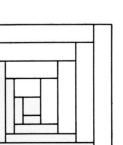 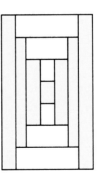

The off-center square is caused by using log strips of two different widths. The Off-Center block is assembled in the same way as the traditional spiraling block.

Patricia Cooper
Middletown, Illinois

Patricia confesses that she has more quilts planned than she will ever complete in her lifetime, but that doesn't stop her from pursuing quilting with energy and enthusiasm. Her quilting plans include not only herself, but also the community of Middletown. She is eager to begin conducting quilting classes in her little country shop in Middletown, and to organize a daytime quilting guild. "People are hungry for new skills here," says Patricia. She belongs to two guilds herself outside Middletown, Quilters at Heart, in Lincoln, Illinois, and Q.U.I.L.T.S., in Springfield, Illinois.

Besides the technical side, Patricia reminds us there is the sociable side to quilting. "I meet many interesting people with common goals and feel that I am also able to touch people's lives at times with my quilting," says Patricia.

Purple Mountain Majesties
1986

After praying for inspiration, Patricia designed this quilt, using the song "America the Beautiful" for a theme. The Log Cabin block is used to form mountains, snow, sky, and clouds in this pictorial quilt of our country's majestic mountain scenery. Depth is created by color choices and arrangement of log strips. Patricia's bearded wheat design for quilting along the cream borders was drawn from an actual wheat stem. *Purple Mountain Majesties* was most recently displayed at the Lincoln Home National Historic Site in Springfield, Illinois, as part of the celebration of the Statue of Liberty centennial and the Fourth of July.

Purple Mountain Majesties

Finished Quilt Size
72" x 72"

Number of Blocks and Finished Size
24 red center blocks—9" x 9" each
12 lavender center
  blocks—9" x 9" each

Fabric Requirements
Reds, purples, blues,
  and browns — 1¼ yd. total
Lavenders, cream,
  pastel blues, and
  pinks — ¾ yd. total
Cream — 2¼ yd.
Rose — 1¾ yd.
Backing — 4½ yd.
Binding — ¾ yd.

Quilt Top Assembly
1. Piece Log Cabin block in the traditional spiraling pattern. Begin with a 1½" square, and add 4 rows of 1½"-wide strips. Piece 24 blocks with red centers and 12 blocks with lavender centers. Refer to the quilt photograph for the proper color arrangement.
2. Arrange blocks in mountain scene before joining. Join blocks into rows of 6. Join rows.
3. Cut 4½"-diameter circle for sun from rose fabric, and appliqué to mountain scene.
4. Cut 4 border strips from rose, 1" wide, join to Log Cabin blocks, and miter corners.
5. Cut 4 border strips from cream, 7½" wide, join to quilt, and miter corners.

Quilting and Finished Edges
Quilt in-the-ditch in sky area and along the contours of the mountains. Wheat quilting pattern is quilted along cream borders. Bind with cream fabric.

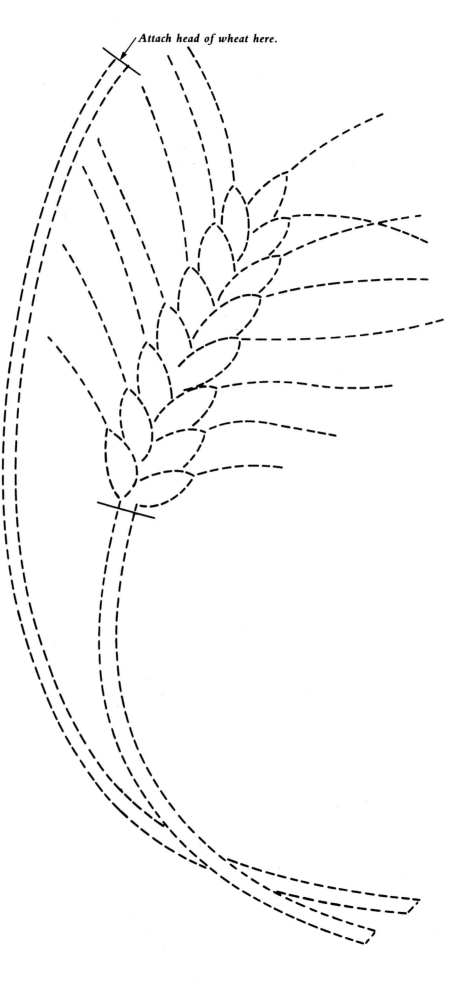

Attach head of wheat here.

Fran Nelson

Fredericksburg, Texas

During the quietness of the evening, they peered through the cracks of the musty chicken coop that they called home, to view the sparkling Texas sky. At that moment, it was hard to believe that same sky was the author of so many relentless days of dust and heat. If this sounds like the beginning of a Texas novel, it's not. Nestled in the center of Texas, Fran and her husband, Leo, have been homesteading for the last six years. "Our home has evolved from tents to chicken coops to cabins, and presently to a half-finished studio and log cabin," says Fran. "I can really sympathize with the pioneer woman."

While her husband built little shelters here and there on the land, Fran put together thousands of pieces of denim for her quilts. "Homesteading and quilting seem to go hand in hand," declares Fran. Her quilts are exclusively denim, mostly from old faded jeans, with some new denim sprinkled in for contrast. Fran admits, "I love the look and feel of faded denim—so soft, yet so strong— with as many different shades as you've got jeans."

Country Fair Day 1986
1986

Why keep you in suspense any longer—*Country Fair Day 1986* was named that because it was exhibited at the San Antonio Stockshow Country Fair Day in 1986! Remarkably, five pairs of old blue jeans and new bleached denim captured the First Prize and Grand Champion ribbons at the country fair. *Country Fair Day 1986* is representative of all the fabulous features of Fran's faded denim quilts. Influenced by the God's Eye design and other Indian weavings, Fran has rotated six rows of graded shades of denim around a pale blue center in the Courthouse Steps fashion. Set diagonally, the Courthouse Steps block is then flanked by stripped-bordered triangles to complete the block. Faithful to the mode of denim jeans, all pieces are secured with topstitching after being joined. Fran's daughter, Jodi Morgano, assisted with this quilt by cutting the strips.

Fran told us to be aware of one thing when working with denim. No matter how precise your stitching, your finished square may be somewhat wider across the center than at the corners. Fran suggests trimming your blocks before joining them.

Country Fair Day 1986

Finished Quilt Size
78″ x 98″

Number of Blocks and Finished Size
12 blocks—17½″ x 17½″ each

Fabric Requirements
Denim shades, beginning with the
lightest:

Shade 1	— ½ yd.
Shade 2	— 2½ yd.
Shade 3	— 1¼ yd.
Shade 4	— 2¾ yd.
Shade 5	— 2¼ yd.
Shade 6	— 2¼ yd.
Shade 7	— 2½ yd.
Chambray for backing	— 8 yd.
Binding (Shade 7)	— 1¼ yd.

Number to Cut
Template A   —144 shade 2
Template B   —48 shade 1

Quilt Top Assembly
1. Piece Log Cabin block in the Courthouse Steps pattern and add 6 rows of 1⅜″-wide strips. Begin with a shade 1 square, 2¼″, and graduate to shade 7, omitting shade 5. The last log strip is a combination of shades 5 and 7 strips. Finished size for Courthouse Steps block is a 12¼″ square. Join 1″-wide strips of shade 5 to the sides of triangle (A). Make 12 for each block. Join 1⅛″-wide strips of shade 7 to the sides of triangle (B). Make 4 for each block. Join stripped triangles so that 1 dark-stripped triangle (B) is framed by 3 light-stripped ones (A). (See block silhouette.) A large triangle is formed. Set Courthouse block diagonally, and join 1 large triangle to each side. All seams are topstitched after joining. Make 12 blocks.
2. Cut 31 sashing strips, 2½″ wide, from shade 7. Add a 1″ x 2½″ rectangle from shade 5 on each end of sashing strip. Alternate 4 sashing strips with 3 blocks, and join, beginning with a sashing strip to form a row. Make 4 block rows.
3. Cut twenty 2½″ accent squares from shade 1. Alternate 3 sashing strips with 4 accent squares, and join, beginning with an accent square to form a sashing row. Make 5 sashing rows.

4. Alternate sashing rows with block rows, and join, beginning with a sashing row.
5. Cut first border strips 2″ wide from shade 6, and join to quilt.
6. Cut second border strips 1¼″ wide from shade 2, and join to quilt.
7. Cut third border strips 3″ wide from shade 7, and join to quilt.
8. Cut fourth border strips 3″ wide from shade 4, and join to quilt.

Quilting
All quilting is done in-the-ditch. Quilt around each center square and every other log strip. Quilt inside each triangle and accent square, and along sashing seam lines.

Finished Edges
Bind with 3½″ denim binding from shade 7.

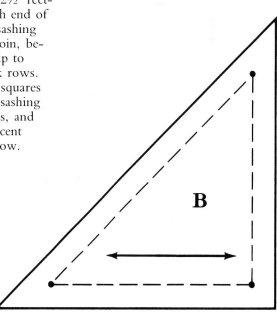

Patti Connor
Collinsville, Illinois

Patti calls quilting "functional art" and, like many artists, creates her masterpieces in a large, bright studio. "It has lots of open shelving, space for several projects at once, and a door that closes!" exclaims Patti. An advantage to living in Collinsville is that Patti can be a member of quilt guilds in two different states. She is an active member of the Heartland Quilters' Guild in Edwardsville, Illinois, and presently Secretary for the Loose Threads Quilt Guild in St. Peters, Missouri. Be sure to read more about Patti and her *Big Black Quilt* in "Quilts Across America."

White Christmas
1986

This quilt was Patti's first piecing project to involve more than a few blocks, and her first exercise in making successive borders fit with each other. The center is composed of one Courthouse Steps Log Cabin block joined to eight traditional spiraling Log Cabin blocks to form a large Christmas wreath in traditional reds and greens. Personalize your Christmas quilt by duplicating your favorite Christmas cookie cutter designs on Patti's spacious white borders and green corner squares.

White Christmas

Finished Quilt Size
60" x 60"

Number of Blocks and Finished Size
1 red/green
  Courthouse Steps block—9" x 9"
4 green/white blocks—9" x 9" each
3 solid green blocks—9" x 9" each
1 solid white block—9" x 9"

Fabric Requirements
Solid red and
  red scraps   —1¼ yd. total
Solid green and
  green scraps   —2 yd. total
White   —1¾ yd.
Backing   —4 yd.
Christmas plaid
  for binding   — ¾ yd.

Number to Cut
Triangle   —100 red scraps
              100 green scraps

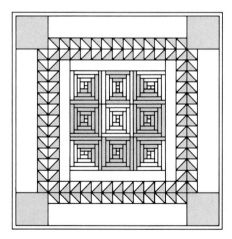

Quilt Top Assembly
1. Piece Log Cabin blocks in the traditional spiraling pattern. Begin with a red 1½" square, and add 4 rows of 1½" strips. Make 4 blocks with green scraps and white, 3 blocks with green scraps, and 1 block with solid white.
2. Piece one Log Cabin block in the Courthouse Steps pattern, using red and green scraps.

3. Arrange blocks in wreath pattern, join blocks into rows, and join rows.
4. Refer to Quilt Piecing Diagram for steps 4 through 8. Cut 2 border strips from white, 3½" x 27½", and 2 border strips, 3½" x 33½". Set aside.

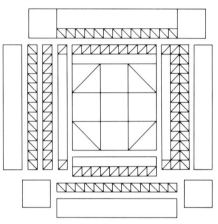

Quilt Piecing Diagram

5. Join each red triangle to a green triangle. Join squares into 2 rows of 9 squares each, and 6 rows of 13 squares each. There will be 4 squares remaining. Paying close attention to the quilt photograph so that red and green squares fall in their proper position, stitch one of the remaining 4 squares to each end of the longer white strips made in step 4.
6. Join lengthwise the rows of 9 squares to the shorter white strips. Join strips to top and bottom of Log Cabin blocks.
7. Join 2 rows of 13 squares each lengthwise, and then join to longer white strip. Repeat for other side. Join to left and right sides of quilt,

being sure to match triangle points.
8. Cut 4 border strips from white, 6½" x 39½". Join a strip to each quilt side. Join a strip to the remaining two 13-square strips made in step 5. Cut four 9½" squares from solid green. Join to ends of unattached strips. Join to quilt.

Quilting
Lay quilt top on a large flat surface, and find the center point of each side unit. Use this as a placement guide to center your first cookie cutter design. Patti used a rope quilting pattern that begins at the corners of the first white strips surrounding the Log Cabin blocks, and reverses direction at the center point. All other quilting is outline quilting, ¼" from seam lines.

Finished Edges
Use 3"-wide bias binding from red-and-green plaid fabric to bind quilt. Attach to quilt, mitering corners, turn to back side, and blind-stitch in place. "Sit back and smile!" suggests Patti.

Marcia Karlin

Highland Park, Illinois

Metamorphosis
1985
The use of intense colors accentuates the clean lines of these off-centered Log Cabin blocks for this mesmerizing display of colors in motion. Metamorphose your scrap bag with this quickie!

A fleece-covered wall in her basement studio is where most of Marcia's quilt designs originate. In two years Marcia has completed 15 quilts, and this from a woman who confesses, "I had never especially enjoyed sewing."

At home all day raising two small children, Marcia realized she had a need to pursue an outside interest. Her first pursuit was studying and collecting antiques, but the guilt of shopping expeditions and filling the house with unnecessary items consumed her. She enrolled in a quiltmaking class, and suddenly a whole world of possibilities and challenges opened up to her. "I responded to the visual and tactile appeal of fabric," says Marcia. "Quilts give me an ongoing sense of accomplishment and deep satisfaction without the guilt associated with collecting antiques. Quilting also allows a sense of autonomy and control that parenting does not permit."

Marcia has engineered some wonderful effects of color in motion by using a variety of fabrics, such as taffetas, decorator chintzes, and Japanese yukata prints, to make quilted wall hangings. Two of these have been included in our "Designer Gallery."

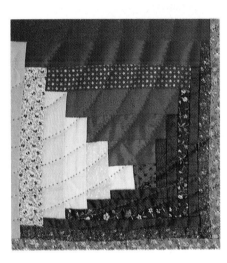

Metamorphosis

Finished Quilt Size
40″ x 40″

Number of Blocks and Finished Size
16 off-centered
   Log Cabin blocks—10″ x 10″ each

Fabric Requirements
Hues of blues, greens,
  grays, and
  purples   —2 yd. total
Hues of reds
  and yellows   —2¼ yd. total
Backing   —1½ yd.
Binding   — ¾ yd.

Quilt Top Assembly
1. Piece off-centered Log Cabin block, beginning with a 1½″ pastel square. Narrow log strips are 1″ wide and from cool hues (blues, greens, grays, and/or purples). Wide log strips are 1½″ wide and from red and yellow hues. Warm colors graduate from the lightest hues in the center to the darkest hues on outside edges. Cool colors move from darkest at center to lightest on outside edges. Marcia suggests laying out all log strips before stitching, to obtain the right color combinations.
2. Join blocks in rows of 4. Join rows.

Quilting and Finished Edges
Refer to Quilting Diagram. Curved quilting lines vary from ¼″ apart, in and around the center, to 1½″ apart for outer curves. Round corners, and bind with gray fabric.

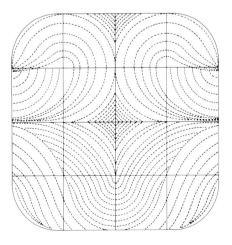

Mountain City Homemakers Club members (left to right)— Cindy Olson, Rosella Chambers, Lou Basanez, Marcia Bieroth, Karan Mori, Wanda Larsen, Janice Connelley, Carol Vaught, and Anna Tremewan—proudly display two of their recent raffle quilts.

Mountain City Homemakers Club

Mountain City, Nevada

Mountain City is a small (75 people) ranching and mining community, sheltered amidst the mountains of the Humboldt National Forest in Nevada. Often, 25 percent of its population are proud members of its Homemakers Club. Begun in 1974, this industrious group of women is not only involved in quilting endeavors, but also in a wide range of community service projects, cookbook publications, and craft shows. Proceeds from cookbook sales are used to fund community center needs and annual Christmas philanthropic programs, as well as to buy quilting materials.

Despite the fact that the nearest fully stocked fabric store is 160 miles away in Boise, Idaho, this group has made 15 quilts in the past 12 years. The first full year of their club's existence, they made a yellow nine-patch quilt to raffle off as a fund raiser. The winner of that first quilt did not live near them, and they never saw the quilt again. To try to prevent their quilts from leaving Mountain City, the group decided the drawing would always be among the members. The number of chances to win the quilt is determined by the number of years the member has belonged to the club, or the number of years since the member has won a quilt. Needless to say, capturing quilts to remain in any domain is difficult at best, but the Homemakers Club hopes the quilting bonds will keep them close by.

Log Cabin Star
1985

A variety of gray-and-black Log Cabin blocks enhances the shocking-pink star medallion of this graphically appealing quilt. With a small battalion of two sewers, two ironers, and two runners, blocks are quickly assembled in one meeting. After blocks are sewn, they are laid out on the floor to check the exact placement. The runners pick up the blocks, take them to the sewer, then to the ironer, and then back to the floor, making sure they remain in proper sequence. Backing and batting are pinned and the quilt is framed and basted to remain in the community hall, so that quilters can come and quilt at their convenience. "Since not every member in the Homemakers Club is a quilter, it is easy to get volunteers to be ironers and runners," explains club member Janice Connelley, "and in addition, every member is contributing to the making of the quilt."

The makers of *Log Cabin Star* were the 11 members of the Homemakers Club for 1985: Anna Tremewan, Lou Basanez, Janice Connelley, Karan Mori, Marcia Bieroth, Donna Nyrehn, Rosella Chambers, Margie Vipham, Wanda Larsen, Cindy Olson, and Carol Vaught.

Log Cabin Star

Finished Quilt Size
84″ x 84″

Number of Blocks and Finished Size
52 gray/black
  blocks—10½″ x 10½″ each
8 pink/black
  blocks—10½″ x 10½″ each
4 pink blocks—10½″ x 10½″ each

Fabric Requirements
Hot pink   — 2¼ yd.
Gray print I   — ⅝ yd.
Gray print II   — 1⅛ yd.
Gray print III   — 1⅝ yd.
Black print I   — 1¼ yd.
Black print II   — 1½ yd.
Black print III — 2 yd.
Backing   — 6 yd.
Binding   — 1¼ yd.

Quilt Top Assembly
1. Piece Log Cabin block in the traditional swirling pattern. Centers are 2″ square; add 3 rows of 2″-wide strips. Make 52 gray-and-black blocks with hot pink centers, starting with strips of light shades and graduating to darker shades for outside edges. Make 8 pink-and-black blocks with black print I as the center fabric. Make 4 solid pink blocks.

2. Assemble blocks into rows and join rows to form the Barn Raising pattern with star medallion. (See quilt photograph.)

Quilting and Finished Edges
Quilt parallel lines, 3½″ apart, outside star medallion from corner to corner, to mimic the diagonal lines of the Log Cabin pattern. Quilt parallel quilting lines, 1½″ apart, following the basic star pattern formed by the star medallion. Bind with hot pink fabric.

Flavin Glover

Auburn, Alabama

Flavin has redefined Log Cabin blocks and patterns in countless ways. Her innovative management of the Log Cabin block has opened doors for her works to be published and exhibited, followed by invitations to lecture and teach workshops. "My identification with Log Cabin designs has enabled me to quickly build a strong, solid reputation in a phase of quilting I had not previously pursued," states Flavin.

Flavin acknowledges that the process is long, especially when working with ½"-wide strips, but the nature of the designs, rather than a time element, dictates the amount of piecing and quilting. "The thought of short-changing techniques in order to be more productive or competitive is a compromise I do not wish to make," says Flavin.

Read more about Flavin and her *Hemlocks* quilt in "Quilts Across America."

Row Houses
1985

If you take a stroll past the row houses of Georgetown, or San Francisco, or Manhattan, it is almost certain that you won't see one made of logs. But look closely at Flavin's row houses, and you'll see two dozen beautiful row houses made from Log Cabin blocks. Flavin designed these houses while the smell of her new house and fresh paint was still in the air. She and her husband had just completed their new house, and after spending hours among numerous color chips of paint in every paint store in town, the design for *Row Houses* instantly came to mind. And naturally, the color chips play a role in the design as well. Circling the houses in a rainbow of shades, color chips echo the colors of the row houses.

Eight Log Cabin blocks are used, to build houses complete with windows, doors, and chimneys. Yardages given are for one-piece borders, so do not hesitate to use the leftover material for windows, chimneys, and strips around color chips. All Log Cabin blocks are the traditional spiraling pattern with 1" log strips and varying center block sizes for window treatment. Flavin's fondness for *Row Houses* is summarized in her statement to us. She says, "Its simplicity and orderliness made it easy to cut, piece, and quilt. It offered hours of sheer enjoyment, as I found it to be stimulating and expressive."

Row Houses

Finished Quilt Size
83" x 104"

Number of Blocks and Finished Size
192 traditional spiraling
  Log Cabin blocks—4½" x 4½"
    each

Maximum Fabric Requirements for One House

Block Area	Rectangle Of Material
Sky	17" x 5"
Roof	17" x 5"
House	40" x 5"
Chimney	1" x 1½"
Windows	8" x 2½"
Door	4" x 5"
Sills and beams (Optional)	4" x 1½"

Fabric Requirements for Quilt With Consolidated Yardages For Houses

Assorted blues	—1¾ yd.
Roof colors	—2 yd.
House colors	—3¾ yd.
Window colors	—⅛ yd.
Chip colors	—½ yd.
Border strips for chips	—1 yd.
Black/gray stripe I	—3 yd.
Black/gray stripe II	—3 yd.
Dusty pink	—2½ yd.
Gray print	—2¾ yd.
Binding	—1¼ yd.
Backing	—6 yd.

Number to Cut

Houses	—24
(8 Log Cabin blocks for each house)	

Template A
(chimney) — 24
Template B
(window) — 19
Template C
(window) — 26
Template D
(window) — 3
Template E
(chips) — 102

Quilt Top Assembly

1. Cut and piece all Log Cabin blocks for each row of houses. Each row house is made from 8 Log Cabin blocks. Each center square or rectangle will indicate by scale the length of each log needed. All blocks will use either 3 or 4 rows of log strips, depending on the house style, and all log widths are 1″ (with seam allowance). Refer to Standard Row House Diagram and notice color alternation for roof and sky blocks. Blocks with a window and/or window and door are mirror images of each other. All "upstairs" window blocks are with 2″ windows (log cabin centers). Flavin's quilt uses a variety of "downstairs" house blocks to change the house style.

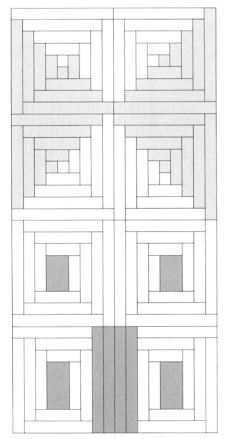

Standard Row House Diagram

Number of house *styles* (not blocks) used are as follows:
Block door,
2½″ window — 6
Stair-step door,
2½″ window — 6
Stair-step door,
2″ sill window — 4
Block door,
2″ sill window — 2
Short block door,
2″ square window — 1½
Short block door,
2½″ window — 1
Block door/beam,
2″ sill window — 3
Block door,
2″ window — 1½
Remember, your windows are your log cabin centers.

House Styles

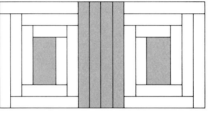

Block door, long window

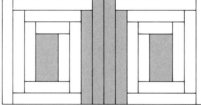

Stair-step door, long window

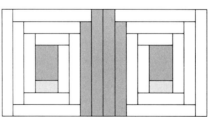

Stair-step door, window with sill

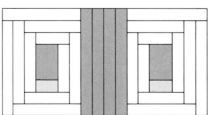

Block door, window with sill

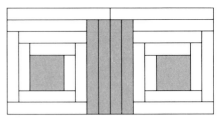

Short block door, square window

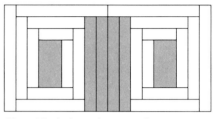

Short block door, long window

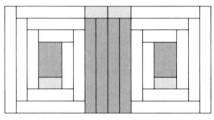

Block door with beam, window with sill

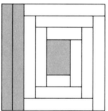

Block door, window

2. Arrange houses into 4 rows of 6 houses, and check for a pleasing color balance before joining. Notice that Flavin has split houses on alternate rows. Join house blocks.
3. Cut 5 sashing strips, 2½″ wide, from black/gray stripe I to attach lengthwise to house rows. Alternate a sashing strip with a house row, and join, beginning with a sashing strip. Cut 2 side sashing strips from black/gray stripe I, 2½″ wide, and join to sides of quilt.
4. Cut 4 border strips, 1″ wide, from black/gray stripe II, join to quilt, and miter corners.
5. Cut 4 border strips, 2″ wide, from dusty pink, join to quilt, and miter corners.
6. Cut 4 border strips, 1″ wide, from black/gray stripe II, join to quilt, and miter corners.

7. Cut color chip squares; border each one with 1"-wide strips from a variety of coordinating colors. Join squares at sides to form border rows, and join to quilt.

8. Cut 4 border strips, 2" wide, from black/gray stripe II, join to quilt, and miter corners.

9. Cut 4 border strips, 2" wide, from gray print, join to quilt, and miter corners.

10. Cut 4 border strips, 2" wide, from black/gray stripe II, join to quilt, and miter corners.

11. Cut 4 border strips, 2¾" wide, from black/gray stripe I, and join to the quilt. (These corners were not mitered.)

Quilting
Outline-quilt along roof edges, between houses, along door strips, and inside windows. Refer to Quilting Diagram for the remainder of Flavin's quilting.

Finished Edges
Bind with black striped fabric.

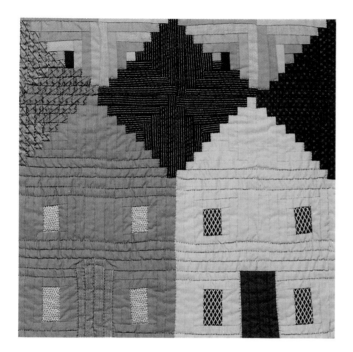

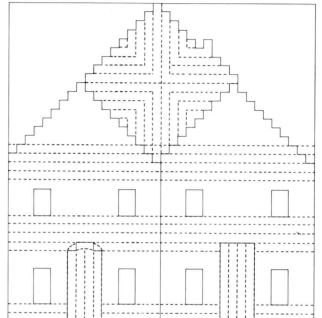

Quilting Diagram

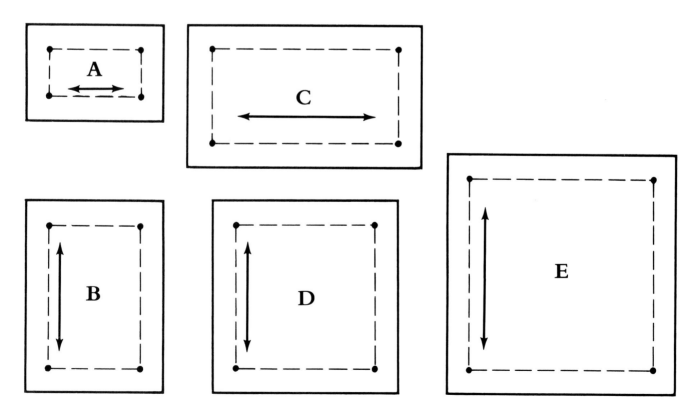

QUILTS ACROSS AMERICA

She pieced scraps of worn-out clothing, too frayed to wear, yet too valuable to throw away. She pieced bits and pieces of filtered memories: her courting days, her wedding, her firstborn child, her husband's weary brow sponged by a sun-bleached sleeve. She quilted them to make layers of warmth for sleeping children. She quilted through tears of joy, through tears of disappointment, and through tears of fatigue. She quilted in rays of sunlight or candlelight, and in crude dwellings, often damp and musty from yesterday's rain. She quilted when there was hope for a better life, and even when there was not. She quilted through plentiful harvests and meager ones. She quilted for her children, for her grandchildren, for neighbors, for nieces and nephews and distant cousins, but rarely for herself. Her quilt was her friend, her confidante, her diary, and part of her self. She left this legacy to the American quilter of today. Her quilting spirit lives on in "Quilts Across America."

Helen Jordan

Norfolk, Virginia

Virginia Wreath
1983

Twelve wreaths with leaves of varying shades of green and yellow surround large red and beige eight-pointed stars on a scalloped field of white. Helen combined her desire to learn to quilt and a talent for design with some fabric she loved very much, to accomplish this wonderful variation of the traditional Bridal Wreath pattern. Starting with that piece of fabric, she matched other fabrics with scraps from her attic, and the quilt grew from that. It was her first quilt, which she started in 1982 and completed in December 1983. "I learned the hard way, by making mistakes and ripping out a lot of stitches. But I was very determined to finish it," states Helen. She made *Virginia Wreath* entirely by hand, and it won a blue ribbon in a local community quilt show. Not bad for a first quilt!

A beginner quilter will find here simple piecing and appliqué techniques, as well as the cutting of scalloped edges. Helen's method for appliquéing was to machine-stitch on the seam line, using this as a guide for turning under the edge. She suggested in her notes to us that quilters may want to try the spray starch method and iron the edge over a cardboard template.

"I hadn't made it for anyone because I didn't realize it would turn out so pretty," says Helen. Well, at the time, Helen might not have made this quilt for anyone in particular, but now she can say she made it for all of us.

At 73, Helen wishes she had started quilting years ago, explaining, "It keeps my mind alert and is like therapy." Even so, in the six years of her quilting career, Helen has progressed to being a quilting teacher, who encourages others to quilt. Today, she enjoys taking traditional patterns and changing them to her own liking. That's a big step from the day when she first began. "I was so inexperienced in quilting that I didn't know you could buy graph paper, so I made my own!"

Helen is an active member of the Tidewater Quilters Guild in Norfolk and also quilts with a group at her church, named the Peacemakers. She has recently ventured into basket weaving and is looking forward to undertaking stained-glass making soon. "I'm finding that at 73 years old, there is still so much to learn," she says. With all this activity in Helen's life, it is easy to see why her latest quilt is for her "dear and patient husband," Eddie.

Virginia Wreath

Finished Quilt Size
Approximately 86″ x 106″, scalloped edges

Fabric Requirements

Solid red	—2 yd.
White	—6 yd.
Beige print	—2 yd.
Green and yellow prints	—⅛ to ¼ yd. each
Solid beige	—½ yd.
Red print for borders and backing	—7 yd.
½″ brown bias tape	—14 yd.
Solid red for binding	—1¼ yd. or 12 yd. bias tape

Number to Cut

Template A	—48 solid red 48 beige print
Template B	—24 solid red 24 beige print
Template C	—12 solid red
Template D	—288 green and yellow prints

Quilt Top Assembly

1. Cut twelve 20½″ squares of white fabric, and fold each in half twice to find center.

2. Make a circle template 13″ in diameter, center it on each white fabric square, and trace the circle.

3. On inside edge of each circle, place edge of brown bias tape, and appliqué to form wreath.

4. For each square, join sides of 8 large diamonds (A), alternating solid red and beige print to form a star. Center star on white square, using fold lines as a guide, and appliqué. Appliqué red circle (C) to star center. Appliqué 24 leaves of various greens and yellows around brown bias circle, to complete wreath. Repeat for each square.

5. Join 3 white squares to form 4 rows. Join rows.

6. Join sides of 8 small diamonds (B), alternating solid red and beige print, to form a star. Center small star at each point where 4 blocks come together, and appliqué. Make 6 small stars, repeat placement, and appliqué.

7. Cut red print border strips 3½″ wide, join to quilt, and miter the corners.

8. Cut white border strips 9½″ wide, join to quilt, and miter the corners.

Quilting

Quilt ⅛″ outside seam line of appliquéd leaves and stars. Quilt ¼″ inside seam line of stars. Center a pair of 1⅝″-diameter circles on each side of white square, 1½″ apart and ⅜″ from edge, and mark for quilting. Set scroll design diagonally in each corner of wreath square, and quilt. Repeat for all wreath squares.

Quilt ⅛″ from each side of border seam lines. Mark swag and flower quilting template for scalloped borders, 1½″ from quilt's edge, and quilt. Five swags should fit along the top and bottom, and seven swags on each side. Adjust swag length to fit around corners. Quilt parallel lines, approximately 2″ apart, to meet swag and flower quilting.

Finished Edges

Trim border to form scallops, and round corners. Helen uses a dinner plate as her scallop-cutting guide. Bind with red fabric.

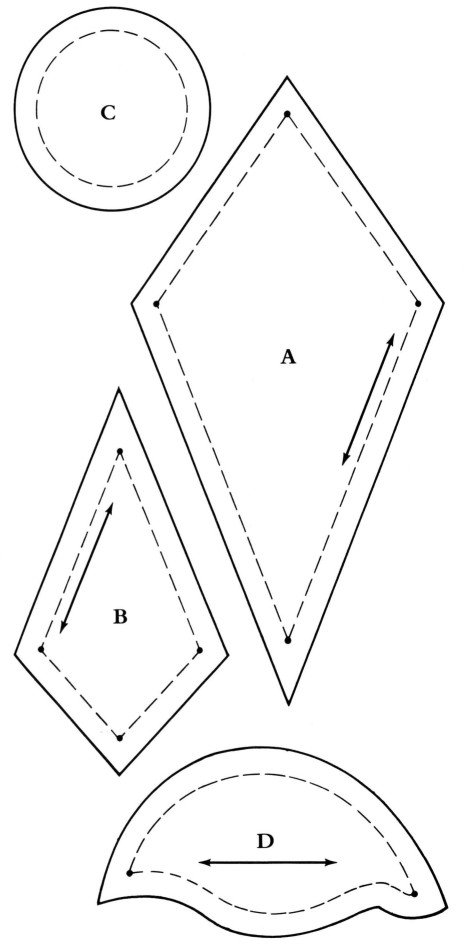

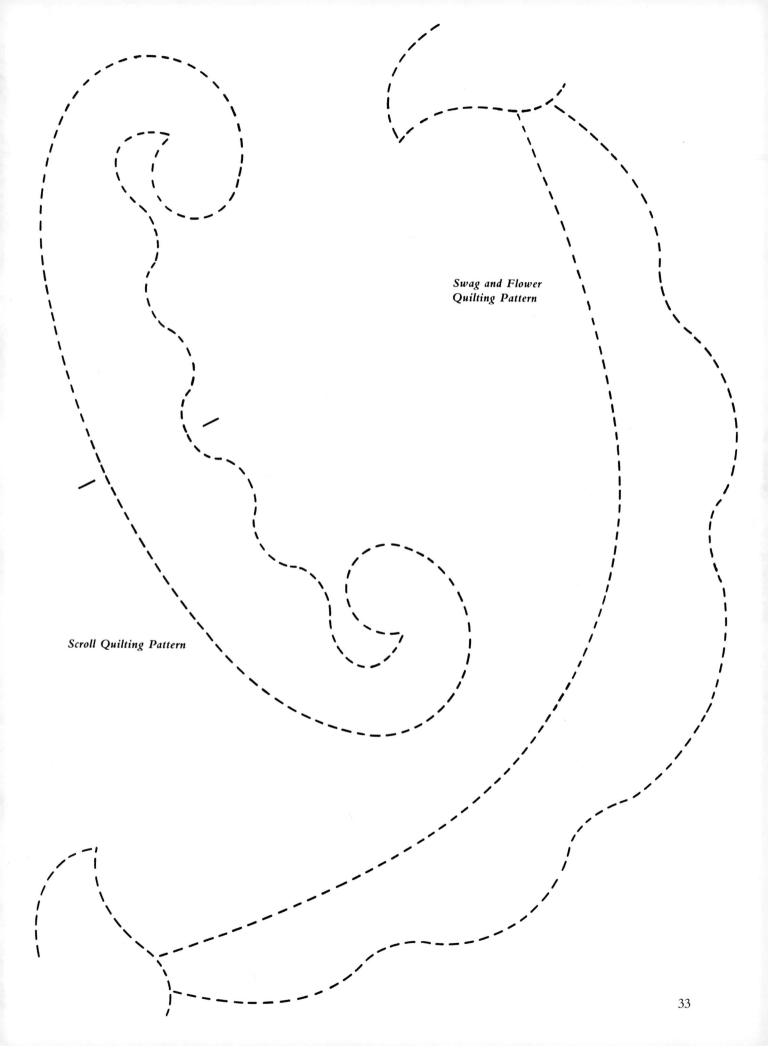

Swag and Flower
Quilting Pattern

Scroll Quilting Pattern

Judy P. Cloninger

Seabrook, Texas

What began as a creative outlet years ago, when Judy decided to stay at home while her children were young, has developed into an all-encompassing activity. "Quilting is my career," proclaims Judy, an honors graduate in economics from the University of South Florida. "My basic goals are to create designs that seem to me beautiful and elegant, and which reflect an enduring, timeless quality." Judy's creating is done at home, where she lives with her husband, Dale, and two sons, Bret and Eric.

For the last four years, Judy has specialized in adapting oriental rug designs to patchwork quilts. "Although I like many traditional patchwork patterns, I've become fascinated by the similarities of American quilts and oriental carpets," says Judy. Her dedication to excellence in quilt design is confirmed by numerous awards for these oriental-style quilts, as well as nationwide teaching invitations.

Persian Illusions
1985

Judy wanted to prove that an oriental design could be simple. Only two pattern pieces are required to develop the optical illusions of *Persian Illusions'* mosaic field. The illusion is produced when light and dark squares and diamonds are alternated, much like the effect produced by the traditional Tumbling Block pattern.

Judy was inspired by the Persian miniatures and floor mosaics in Islamic architecture. The center mosaic field and pieced border replicate the turbans worn by the men and the flat-topped tents they lived in. *Persian Illusions* won the 1985 Award of Merit in the Master's Division, American/International Judged Show, and is completely hand-pieced and hand-quilted.

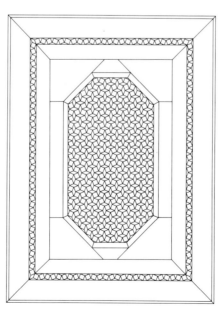

Persian Illusions

Finished Quilt Size
68" x 91"

Fabric Requirements
For pieced mosaic field and border:
Dark prints	—1½ yd. total
Medium prints	—1½ yd. total
Light prints	—2 yd. total

For background:
Medium print	—1¼ yd.

For print borders:
Floral stripe	—4 yd.

(with same border repeated 3 times across width of fabric)

For strip-pieced borders:
Medium prints and stripes	—2½ yd. each
For backing	—6 yd.

Number to Cut

Template A — 182 dark prints
                    187 light prints
Template B — 124 dark prints
Template C — 132 light prints
Template D — 452 medium prints
Template E — 4 background
                    medium print
Template F — 2 background
                    medium print
Template G — 2 background
                    medium print

Quilt Top Assembly

1. Piece center mosaic field by joining diamonds (A) to squares (D) into diagonal rows, starting with the upper right-hand corner. (See Mosaic Piecing Diagram.) Be alert to color choice of diamonds (A). When a diamond is pieced horizontally, it is from light fabrics. When it is pieced vertically, it is from dark fabrics. This is true for piecing throughout the quilt. Judy suggests laying out your mosaic field before joining, to obtain the most pleasing color arrangement. Join rows to form an elongated octagon. (Edges will be uneven.) For piecing accuracy, Judy prefers hand-piecing rows together.

2. Sew horizontally 5 light-colored diamonds (A) to each upper and lower diagonal edge of the mosaic field. The diamond shape should fit nicely between rows. (See photograph and Whole Quilt Diagram.)

3. Make a stripped border for the mosaic field, consisting of 3 strips of fabric—1" wide, 1¼" wide, and ⅞" wide. Finished size of border should be 1⅝" wide. Stripped border should be sewn to mosaic field so that diamonds along the edges of the mosaic field are halved. Corners are mitered. Notice that four very small triangular shapes are formed at the top and bottom corners of the mosaic field when borders are added. (See photograph of quilt.) Finished measurements for Judy's mosaic field are 28" at its widest point and 10½" at the base and top. Cut excess fabric from mosaic field even with the ¼" seam allowance of border.

4. Before joining background fabric, Judy suggests cutting your background templates (E, F, and G) with generous seam allowances, because this is the time to make any adjustments to prevent your finished quilt from being something

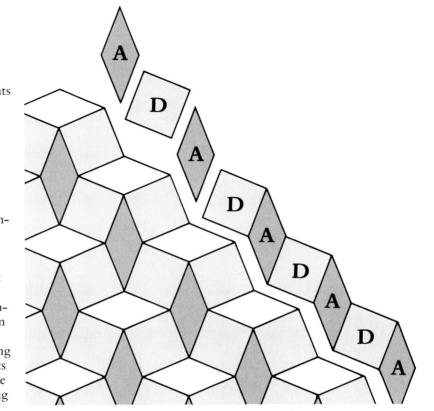

Mosaic Piecing Diagram

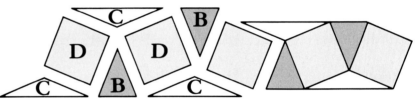

Border Piecing Diagram

other than a rectangle! Lay corner pieces (E), bar pieces (F), and side bar pieces (G) around the bordered mosaic field. Measure your expected finished rectangle. Join side bar strips first, and then corner and short bar pieces.

5. Here you will need to make a choice about border technique. Judy has chosen to remain true to oriental rug designs, and make her side strips for this next border wider than the top and bottom strips. Many oriental rug designs are done this way to widen or expand the rug. If you choose this method, mitered corners are not possible. Cut strips for top and bottom, 4½" wide, and strips for sides, 5¼". Join top and bottom strips first, and then side strips.

If you would like mitered corners and borders of identical widths, cut all strips 4½" wide, join strips to background rectangle, and miter corners.

6. The pieced border consists of a series of basic units as follows: Join a square (D) to the 2 equal sides of triangle (B). Join 1 half-diamond (C) to the top of each square to form the basic unit. (See Border Piecing Diagram.) Connect basic units with template C at the bottom edge of each square, and triangle (B) at top edge. Use one dark-colored vertical diamond (A) to join the horizontal and vertical borders in each of the 4 corners. (See quilt photograph.) Again, you may wish to lay out your pieces before joining, to obtain the best color arrangement.

7. Cut border strips from print fabric, 5¼" wide, join to quilt, and miter corners.

8. Add a stripped border made with the same fabrics as the border that framed the mosaic field. Strips measure 1¼", 1⅛", and 1" wide. Join strips to quilt and miter corners.

Quilting

Quilt in-the-ditch of the diamonds and squares, for mosaic field and pieced border. Follow the lines of fabric designs in print borders, for interesting quilting patterns. Space 6 latch-hook patterns 1″ apart on background fabric, along the diagonal edge of corners (E) and short bars (F). Quilt V pattern as shown on template E. Evenly space double-triangle pattern on the background fabric along side bars (G).

Finished Edges

Bind with dark fabric.

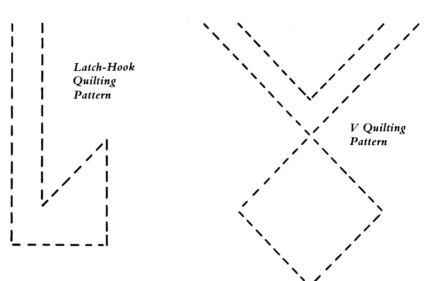

Latch-Hook Quilting Pattern

V Quilting Pattern

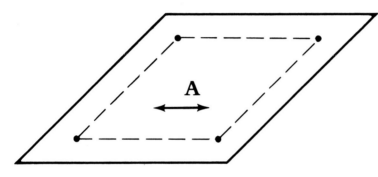

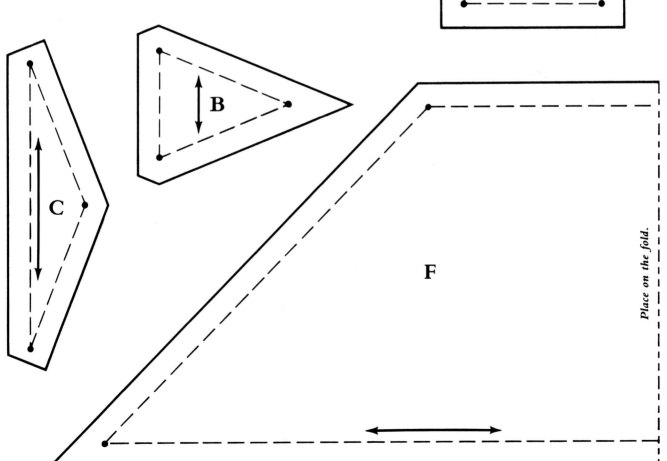

Place on the fold.

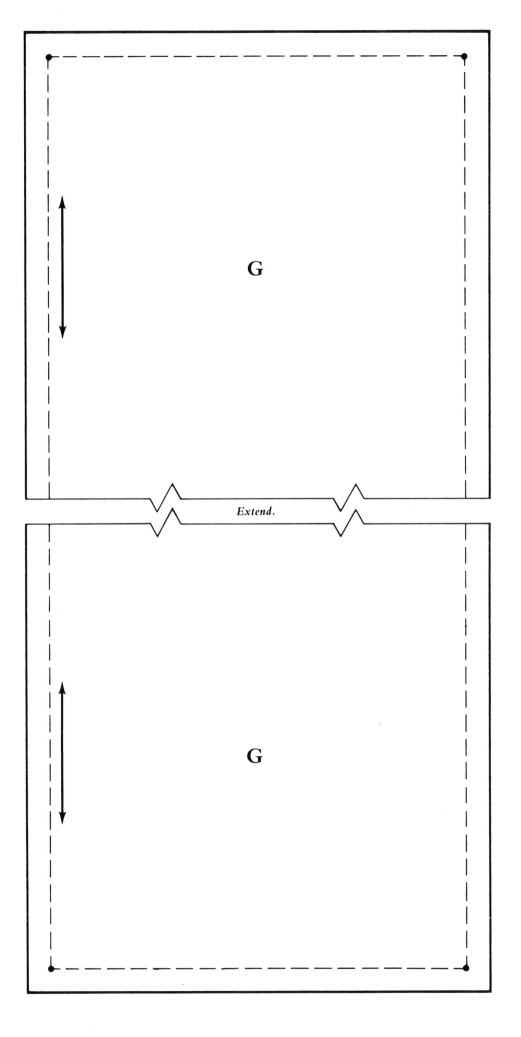

Extend.

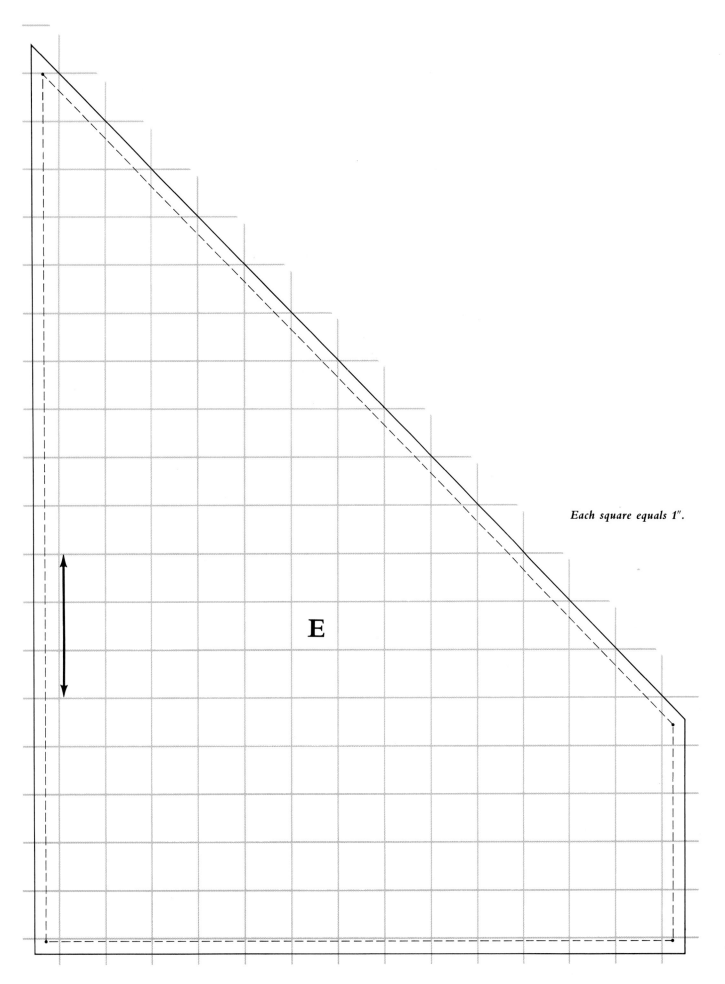

E

Each square equals 1".

Watermelon Patch
1983

From the South to the North, watermelons tell us that summer has arrived. Childhood memories of eagerly waiting at shaded picnic tables for that first slice of cold watermelon are shared by many. Anticipation grows when the knife first cuts the rind: Will this one be red or pink inside? Watermelons remind us of family gatherings, the Fourth of July, bare feet, and outdoor games. *Watermelon Patch* is a wall hanging that will keep those happy times fresh all year.

Three watermelons are appliquéd, using three different red print fabrics to imitate the varying shades of melon. Four different green print fabrics for the leaves add to the quilt's down-home charm. Just as a watermelon vine meanders through the patch, this realistic vine-quilting pattern can meander freely over the quilt. The simple pattern and small size make this just the quilt to start on a cold wintry evening and complete in time to cut that first watermelon of summer.

Jane Eakin
Wilmette, Illinois

As the saying goes—you can take the girl out of the country but you can't take the country out of the girl—and this is true for Jane Eakin. Jane has left the country, where she grew up. But she still loves it, and expresses that love for folk art and country living in her quilts. Wall hangings are her favorites, since they are quick and easy and they place the quilt in full view for everyone to see.

Getting an idea and developing a quilt are the most exciting parts of quiltmaking, according to Jane. Maybe that's why all her designs are originals! A bulletin board full of her quilting ideas hangs in a remodeled 1920s-vintage sleeping porch that she uses as her quilting room.

Before she began quilting, Jane collected quilts. That has made her sensitive to the historical significance of her quilting today. "Quilts are a continuing chain of history; I hope my quilts are treasured by future generations," says Jane.

We enjoyed selecting two quilt designs by Jane which exemplify those qualities of life that Jane treasures. She was assisted with her appliqué and quilting by Ka Yang and Ruth Bell for the *Watermelon Patch* quilt, and Phyllis Sylvester, Emma D. Yoder, and Vivian Walsh for *Hens A-Peckin'*.

Watermelon Patch

Finished Quilt Size
39½" x 47½"

Fabric Requirements
Black — ¼ yd.
Green prints
4 different prints — ½ yd. each
Solid green — 1⅝ yd.
Red prints
2 different prints — ¼ yd. each
1 different print — 1½ yd.
Light print
for background — 1½ yd.
Solid white — 1½ yd.
Muslin for backing — 1½ yd.

Number to Cut
Watermelon — 3 red prints

Watermelon	
rind	—3 white
	3 green prints
Leaves	—8 green prints
Seeds	—60 black

Quilt Top Assembly
1. Cut white background fabric 34½" x 42½". Fold in half twice, finger-crease to find center, and mark.
2. Cut watermelon seeds on bias and appliqué to each red melon, spacing them evenly along bottom curve, ½" from seam line.
3. Use center mark on background fabric to position middle red melon. Do not appliqué at this time. Baste or gluestick white rind to background fabric, using red melon as a

positioning guide. Hand-appliqué red melon and green rind *to white rind*. Then, appliqué entire melon to background.
4. Appliqué remaining 2 melons in same manner, spacing them 1¼" from center melon.
5. Using tendril guideline and ½"-wide bias strips, appliqué 4 tendrils to background. Appliqué leaves over one end of the tendrils, using a different print for leaves at the top of quilt from those at the bottom. Appliqué remaining 6 leaves around the melons, as shown in the photograph of Jane's quilt.
6. Strip-piece border with colors in the following order and widths: green—1¼" wide, white—1" wide, and red print—2" wide. Join to

quilt and miter corners, leaving 1¼"
of red print free to make a rolled
hem when quilting is completed.

Quilting

Randomly place vine-quilting template on quilt top and mark fabric.
Draw freehand quilting lines to
connect vines. Outline-quilt 1/16"
outside seam lines of leaves, tendrils, green rind, watermelons, and
green border. For each red melon,
using red quilting thread, quilt 2
rows of the watermelon seed shape,
½" apart and ½" above row of
black seeds. Space seeds evenly
along the row.

Finished Edges

Turn 1¼" of red print border to
back, turn edge under ¼", and secure with a slipstitch.

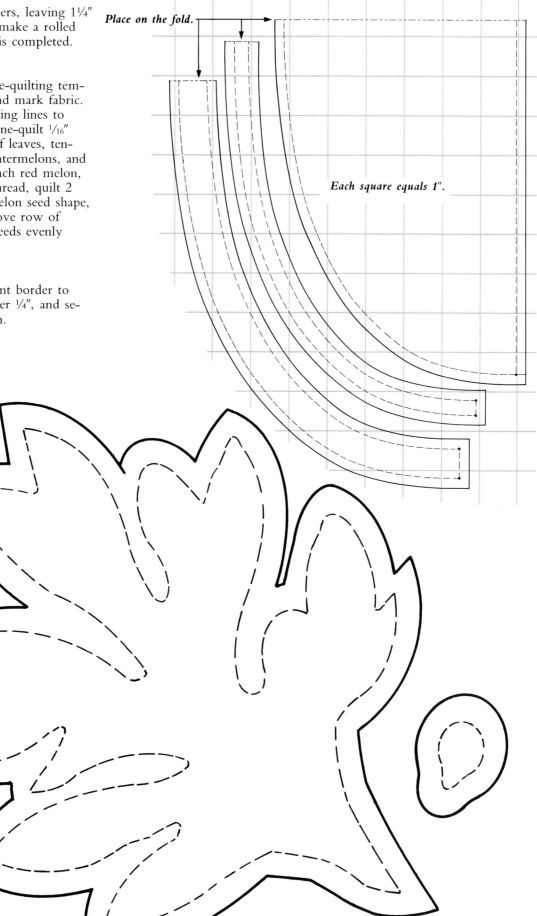

Place on the fold.

Each square equals 1".

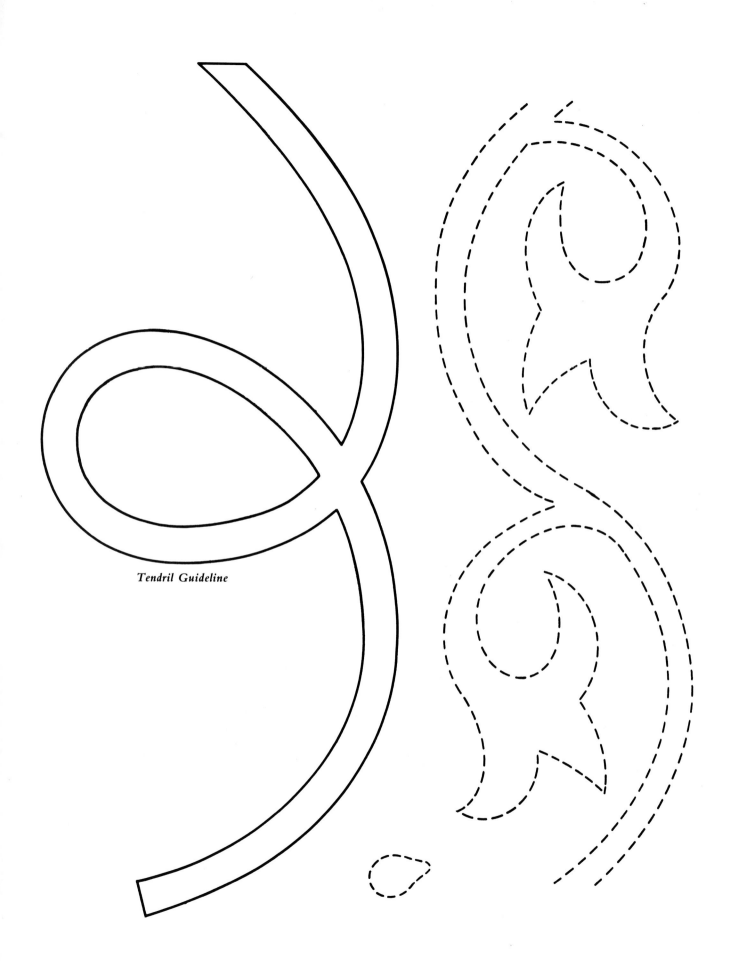

Tendril Guideline

43

Hens A-Peckin'
1985

If the checkerboard pattern on this quilt reminds you of old feed sacks, then we know where you spent your childhood! Anyone who has fed chickens and gathered eggs can relate to Jane's inspiration for this wall hanging. Jane called henhouse duty one of her chores while growing up on a farm. But certainly, she reserved some pleasant reflections to allow her to design such a light-hearted quilt.

Seminole strip piecing is used to create the checkerboard sashing, and the large white chicken is one appliquéd piece. Simple outline quilting, along with a few quilting details on the chicken, makes this wall hanging as easy to do as scrambling eggs!

Hens A-Peckin'

Finished Quilt Size
44" x 44"

Fabric Requirements

Red print	—1½ yd.
White	—2¼ yd.
Gold	— ⅜ yd.
Tan	—1¼ yd.
Blue	— ⅛ yd.
Navy print for binding	—1¼ yd.
Muslin for backing	—3 yd.

Number to Cut

Chicken	—9 white
Comb	—9 gold
Beak	—9 gold
Feet	—9 gold
Square	—4 blue
	12 red print

Quilt Top Assembly
1. Cut nine 11¾" squares from red print fabric. Embroider eye on each chicken. Center one chicken on each red square and appliqué, leaving unsewn those areas where the comb, feet, and beak will be. Appliqué comb, feet, and beak to red square. Repeat for all 9 squares.
2. To make checkerboard sashing, strip-piece strips 1¼" wide of tan, white, and tan; and strips of white, tan, and white. Cut across strips to make 1¼" pieces. Join pieces with a ¼" seam allowance, alternating colors to form ¾" checkerboard squares. Each sash is 15 squares long. Make 24.
3. Alternate 4 checkerboard sashing strips with 3 chicken squares to form a row, beginning with a sashing strip. Make 3 rows.
4. Make 2 rows of sashing and squares in following order: 1 red print square, 1 sashing strip, 1 blue square, 1 sashing strip, 1 blue square, 1 sashing strip, and 1 red print square.
5. Make sashing rows for the top and bottom of the quilt by alternating 4 red print squares with 3 sashing strips.
6. Alternate sashing rows with chicken rows, and join.

Quilting
Quilt feathers on each chicken. You might want to use red quilting thread as Emma Yoder did. Outline-quilt ¼" outside seam line of chicken, and ¹⁄₁₆" outside long seam lines of checkerboard sashing. Quilt a straight line from corner to corner of red and blue sashing squares to form a large X.

Finished Edges
Bind with 2½" double-folded bias of navy print fabric.

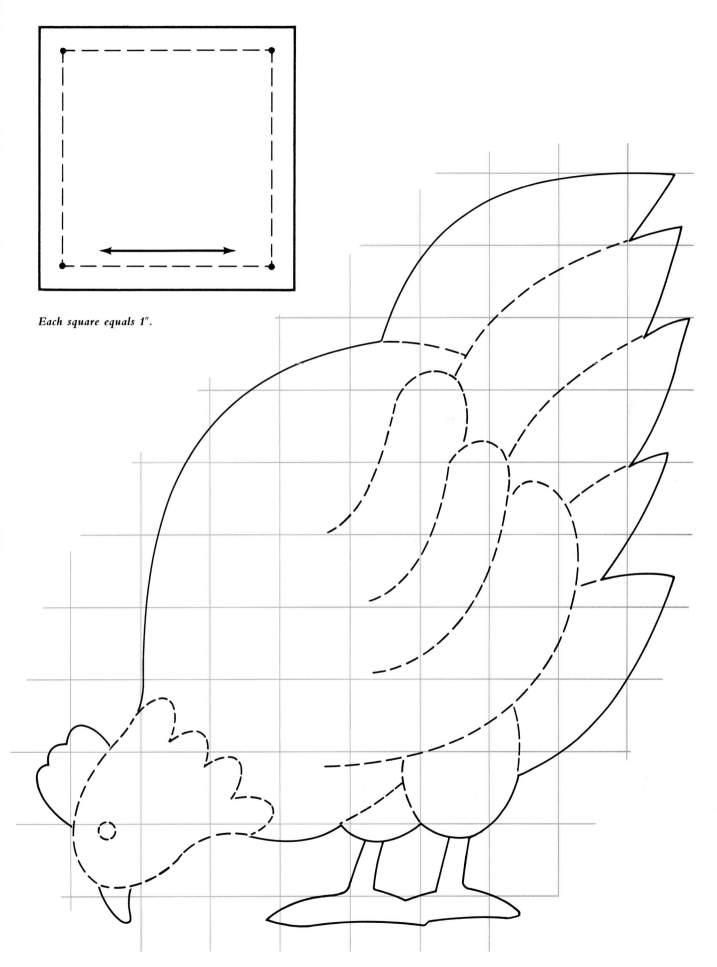

Each square equals 1".

Oak Leaf
1983

Every quilter will appreciate and revere Ethel's precisely stitched appliquéing and hand quilting, exemplified on this quilt. It is easy to understand why it is among Ethel's blue ribbon winners. Appliqué is her favorite type of handwork, and she likes to use the needle-turned method, which requires no basting. Ethel has been commissioned to do another quilt just like *Oak Leaf*, so it must have been someone else's favorite, too.

Ethel Hickman

Camden, Arkansas

In 14 years of quilting, Ethel Hickman has made 25 quilts and won 15 awards. She has been a seamstress for most of her 73 years, but now quilting is her one and only love. Her awards for quilting include Best of Show, Viewer's Choice, and First Place ribbons. Her *Ann Orr's Ye Old Sampler* has recently been selected for the permanent collection of The American Quilter's Society Museum in Paducah, Kentucky. Ethel loves to compete and no wonder, since she usually receives a blue ribbon. She prefers traditional designs, and especially enjoys making white-on-white quilts, having designed six. None of her quilts are for sale.

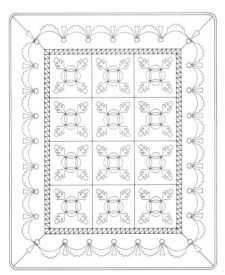

Oak Leaf

Finished Quilt Size
85″ x 103″

Number of Blocks and Finished Size
12 blocks—18″ x 18″ each

Fabric Requirements
Red print   —3 yd.
Green print   —3 yd.
Muslin   —9½ yd.
Muslin for backing
   and binding   —8 yd.

Number to Cut
Template A   —12 red print
Template B   —48 red print
Template C   —48 green print
Template D   —28 red print
Template E   —28 green print

Quilt Top Assembly
1. Cut twelve 18½″ squares from muslin. Finger-crease blocks from corner to corner, to find center and to make guidelines for oak leaves. Mark lightly for oak leaf design placement.
2. Appliqué red center pieces and oak leaves to each block. Ethel uses the needle-turned method of appliqué, with the appliqué stitch and matching thread.
3. Join these oak leaf blocks in 4

rows of 3 blocks. Join rows.
4. Make a sawtooth border with 2″ squares, made from red print and muslin triangles. Ethel suggests the easy machine-piecing method for pieced triangles. Cut red print and muslin in rectangles, 18″ x 22″. Lay the muslin rectangle over the red print rectangle. Mark a 3″ grid on the muslin. Draw diagonal lines through squares. Machine-stitch ¼″ on either side of the diagonal lines. Cut along marked lines. You should have 36 squares of red and muslin triangles. Continue in this manner until you have made 130 squares. Join squares to make 2 rows of 37 squares each, and 2 rows of 28 squares each. Join sawtooth borders to quilt.
5. Cut 4 muslin border strips, 14″ wide, join to the quilt, and miter the corners.
6. Mark border for swag and bell appliqué, so that bottom of bell measures 5½″ from outside edge of quilt. Seven bells with swags

should fit nicely along opposite sides, and 5 bells with swags along the top and bottom borders. Center 1 bell over miter seam for each corner. Cut swags with generous seam allowances on the ends, since Ethel recommends that any adjustments in fitting the swags and bells be made at the ends of the swags. Appliqué border.

Quilting
Outline-quilt along outside edge of all appliquéd pieces. Quilt in-the-ditch of triangle seam lines of saw-tooth border. Quilt background of each block in a 2″ grid, set perpendicularly. Extend parallel lines from 2″ grid across background of 14″ border, and quilt. Parallel lines will meet at a 90° angle at the mitered seam line.

Finished Edges
Round quilt corners, and bind with muslin.

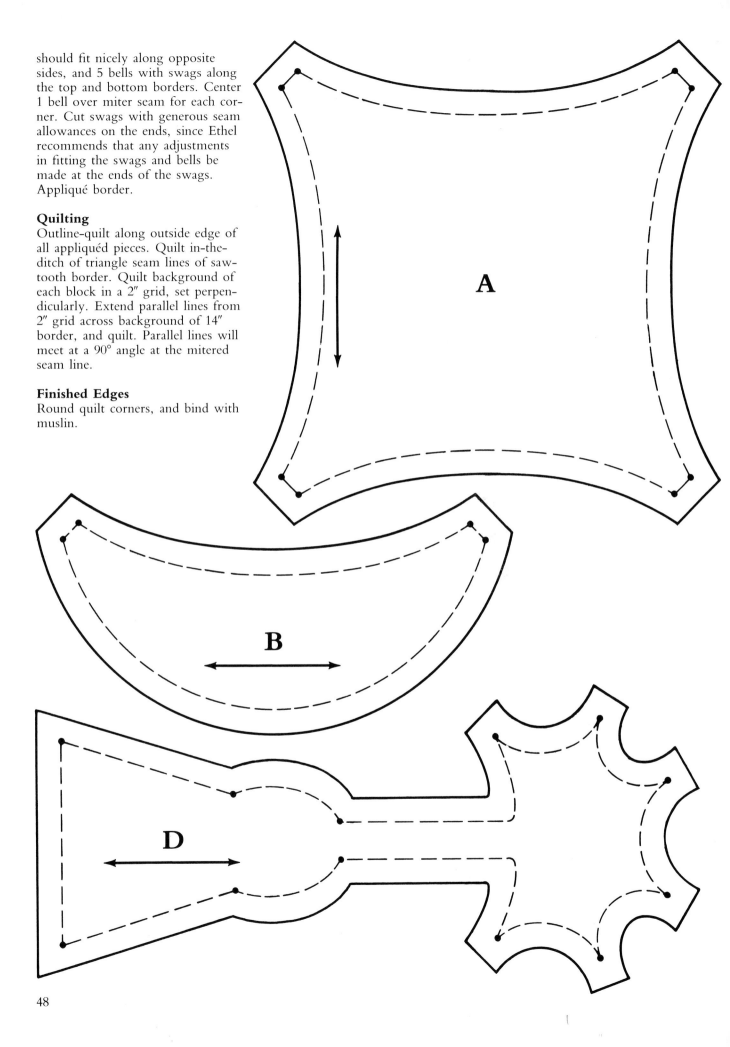

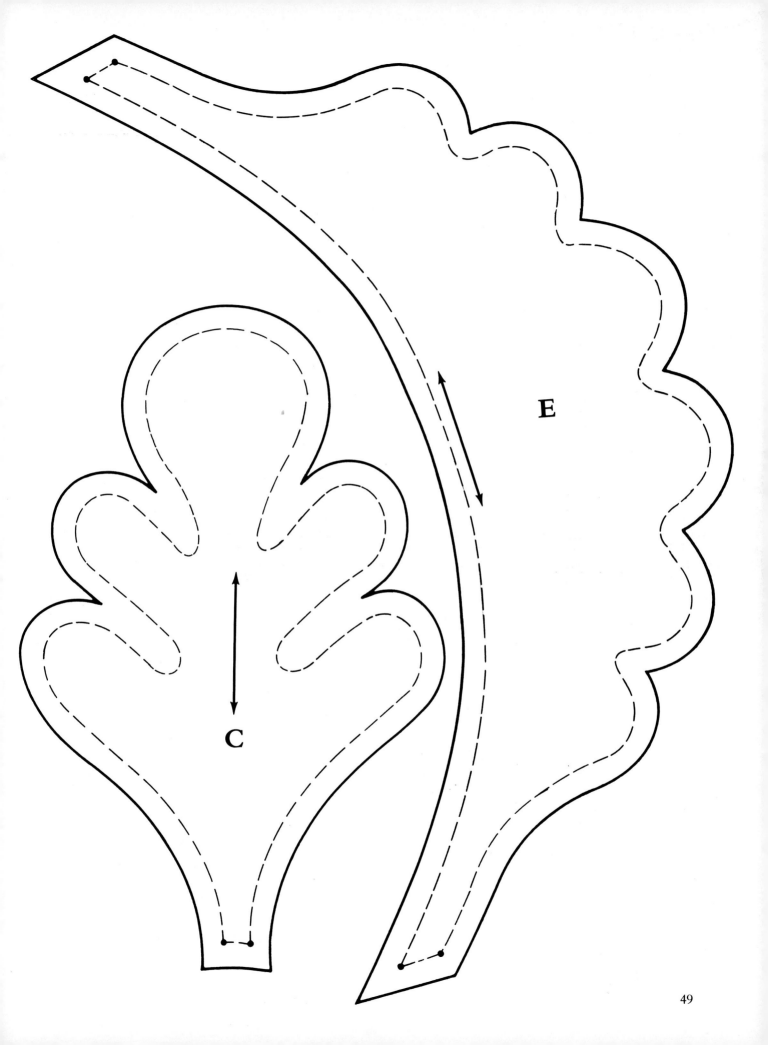

C

E

Arabesque I Jacket
1982

This was Christine's first garment that incorporated the Drunkard's Path block. "A wall hanging I had made with Drunkard's Path looked somewhat like a cape, so it hit me that this pattern should work for a garment. And it has!" explains Christine. She has taken the Drunkard's Path block and turned and mated it with other blocks to form half-circles and full circles down the front and back of this jacket.

Christine likes to have her quilting show inside her garments as well as outside. If you prefer to use a separate lining, you will need to purchase additional material for the lining. Therefore, the red material listed as backing in the directions becomes an interlining.

Christine L. Hile

Valley Falls, Kansas

Christine learned to quilt some six years ago, but her deep interest in quilting didn't begin until she started designing quilts and quilted garments about a year later. "When I found that I could create gorgeous original designs for the wall, and even as wearable art, I found a beautiful new way to express the beauty I feel, and then can share with others," says Christine. "I learned to sew as a child, for my dolls. Creating lovely clothing was a unique talent, so I could 'shine.'"

Christine is quickly becoming famous for the ingenious ways she has manipulated Drunkard's Path into coats, capes, and jackets. She likes keeping her one-of-a-kind designs fun and innovative, to appeal to all quilters. Directions for Christine's garments are given for a small size, but by increasing the number of blocks along the underarm and side seams, they can easily be adjusted to whatever size you need.

Arabesque III Coat
1984

Christine decided to let 219 Drunkard's Path blocks run (stagger) across the front and back of this full-length coat. Its oriental style makes it adaptable to casual as well as formal wear.

As above, if you prefer a separate lining, you will need to purchase additional material for the lining. Therefore, the black print material listed as backing in the directions becomes an interlining. The length of the coat can be adjusted by adding or subtracting rows of blocks on the lower edges of the back and front panels.

Front

Arabesque I Jacket

Jacket Size
8

Number of Blocks and Finished Size
140 Drunkard's Path
  blocks—3″ x 3″ each

Fabric Requirements
Black	—1¼ yd.
Black print	—3 yd.
Red for backing	—2 yd.

Number to Cut
Template A	—140 black
Template B	—140 black print

Jacket Assembly
1. Piece 140 Drunkard's Path blocks, being sure to align curve marks.

Back

2. Join blocks at sides to make jacket rows, as shown in jacket diagram. Join rows to form 3 jacket sections: 2 front panels and back. Christine suggests numbering small squares of paper, and pinning one to the first block in each row. This eliminates having to remember which row you are working on.

Quilting
Outline-quilt ¼" inside curved seam line of template A.

Final Assembly
Machine-stitch shoulder seams with a ¼" seam allowance, matching blocks and pinning frequently to control slippage. Trim batt within seams, and finger-crease seams open. Using bias strips made from black print, cover seams, turn each edge under ¼", and whipstitch into place. Machine-stitch underarm and sleeve seams with ¼" seam allowance, sewing from lower edge to underarm and locking stitch. Remove garment from machine. Machine-stitch from outer sleeve edge to underarm and lock stitch. Carefully clip seams at underarm. Trim batt, and cover seams with bias strips as before. Apply black print bias edging in following order: bottom edge, neck, front edges, and sleeve edges.

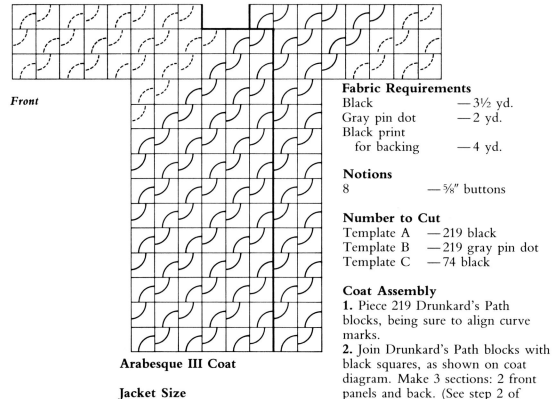

Front

Arabesque III Coat

Jacket Size
8

Number of Blocks and Finished Size
219 Drunkard's Path
blocks—3" x 3" each

Fabric Requirements
Black   —3½ yd.
Gray pin dot   —2 yd.
Black print
    for backing   —4 yd.

Notions
8   —⅝" buttons

Number to Cut
Template A   —219 black
Template B   —219 gray pin dot
Template C   —74 black

Coat Assembly
1. Piece 219 Drunkard's Path blocks, being sure to align curve marks.
2. Join Drunkard's Path blocks with black squares, as shown on coat diagram. Make 3 sections: 2 front panels and back. (See step 2 of Jacket Assembly.)

Quilting
Quilt in-the-ditch of Drunkard's Path seam lines. Repeat Drunkard's Path curve on black squares.

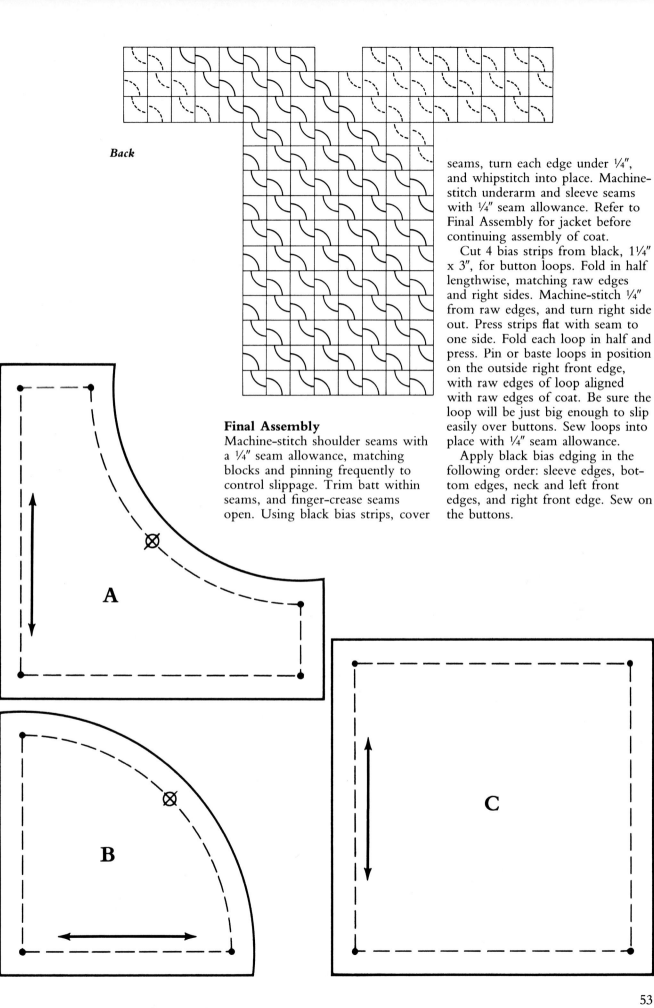

Back

Final Assembly
Machine-stitch shoulder seams with a ¼″ seam allowance, matching blocks and pinning frequently to control slippage. Trim batt within seams, and finger-crease seams open. Using black bias strips, cover seams, turn each edge under ¼″, and whipstitch into place. Machine-stitch underarm and sleeve seams with ¼″ seam allowance. Refer to Final Assembly for jacket before continuing assembly of coat.

Cut 4 bias strips from black, 1¼″ x 3″, for button loops. Fold in half lengthwise, matching raw edges and right sides. Machine-stitch ¼″ from raw edges, and turn right side out. Press strips flat with seam to one side. Fold each loop in half and press. Pin or baste loops in position on the outside right front edge, with raw edges of loop aligned with raw edges of coat. Be sure the loop will be just big enough to slip easily over buttons. Sew loops into place with ¼″ seam allowance.

Apply black bias edging in the following order: sleeve edges, bottom edges, neck and left front edges, and right front edge. Sew on the buttons.

A

B

C

Baltimore Wreath
1983

Baltimore Wreath contains four navy-and-cream appliquéd blocks based on a wreath from the famous *Baltimore Bride's Quilt* of 1850. Wreath blocks are enhanced by latticework borders. Inspiration to arrange a quilt in this fashion came from a 1981 issue of *Quilter's Newsletter* (see our Resource Section for more details). However, the design, color selection, and arrangement, including the prairie points, are Martha's. This was the first quilt Martha organized herself, worked on by herself, and quilted alone. She always uses prairie points on the finished edges of her quilts. She considers them her trademark. "I use them in different sizes to complement my piece," says Martha. "They seem to add just the right finishing touch."

Martha Street
Winterset, Iowa

Living in the country, her family, and quilting are a few of Martha's loves. She and her husband of 40 years operate an auto repair and body shop near Winterset. But besides this, Martha is often able to squeeze 10 to 15 hours of quilting into a week. Martha tells us all of her family are "crafty" and like to do things with their hands. "I'm not one to tell too much about myself," admits Martha, "but I do enjoy talking about my quilting." She gains much pleasure by challenging herself to improve her designs, by variations in the color, the design, or the arrangement. "I especially like the comments and points made when my work is judged," explains Martha. "This helps me improve my workmanship for the next project."

Baltimore Wreath

Finished Quilt Size
Approximately 82″ x 93″

Number of Blocks and Finished Size
4 Wreath blocks—19″ x 21″ each

Fabric Requirements
Navy print — 4¾ yd.
  (without prairie
  points) — 3¾ yd.
Beige — 5¼ yd.
  (includes yardage
  for bias strips)
Red/navy floral
  stripe — 3¾ yd.
Navy paisley stripe — 2¾ yd.
Backing — 5½ yd.

Number to Cut
Template A — 16 beige
Template B — 16 navy paisley
              stripe

Template C — 32 beige
              96 red/navy
              floral stripe
Template D — 32 beige
Template E — 32 beige
Template F — 36 navy
Template G — 18 beige
Template H — 9 beige

Quilt Top Assembly
1. Cut 4 rectangles from navy print, 19½″ x 21½″. Fold each in half twice to find center, and once more to find diagonal placement lines, and mark. Martha believes it is important to add the latticework before appliquéing. Appliquéing seems to shrink the blocks, and adding the latticework provides a more even background. Cut 12 strips, 1½″ x 19½″, and 12 strips, 1½″ x 21½″, from beige fabric for latticework. Cut 6 strips, 4½″ x 19½″, from red/navy floral stripe, and 6 strips, 4½″ x 21½″. Join lengthwise 2 beige lattice strips of equal length with 1 floral-stripe strip in the middle. Make 12.
2. Piece lattice blocks, using templates F, G, and H. Make 9.
3. Alternate 3 lattice blocks with ends of two 19½″ lattice strips, and join, beginning with a lattice block. Make 3 rows.

4. Alternate three 21½″ lattice strips with sides of 2 navy blocks, and join, beginning with a lattice strip. Make 2 rows.

5. Join rows by alternating a lattice block row with a navy block row to complete center block section.

6. Center and draw a 12″-diameter circle in each navy block. Pin a 1″-wide bias strip along circle line, turning under ¼″ on each side for seam allowance, and press. Use bias circle for positioning all other pieces before appliquéing, and the diagonal placement lines to position the 4 groups of 3 bias stems. Template D leaves are placed on inside edge of wreath. Martha suggests pinning all 4 wreaths in place before appliquéing, so that all 4 will be exactly the same. Appliqué wreaths, sewing bias circle last. Notice that, for variation, Martha appliquéd 24 beige leaves on 2 blocks, and 20 beige leaves on the other 2.

7. Cut 2 border strips, 2″ wide, from beige fabric. Join to top and bottom of quilt. (Those who, like Martha, do not like square quilts will enjoy this step!)

8. Cut 4 border strips, 2¼″ wide, from floral stripe, join to quilt, and miter corners.

9. Cut 4 border strips, 1⅞″ wide, from beige fabric, join to quilt, and miter corners.

10. Cut 4 border strips, 4¾″ wide, from navy fabric, join to quilt, and miter corners.

11. Cut 4 border strips, 2½″ wide, from beige fabric, join to quilt, and miter corners.

12. Cut 4 border strips, 2¼″ wide, from navy paisley stripe, join to quilt, and miter corners.

13. Cut 4 border strips, 1″ wide, from beige fabric, join to quilt, and miter corners.

Quilting

Outline-quilt along outside edge of appliquéd wreaths and beige lattice-work. Martha chose a floral vine pattern for her lattice blocks and beige and navy border strips. She mimicked the paisley shape of her border strips and quilted them on her last beige border. Outline-quilt along floral and paisley patterns of border strips.

Finished Edges

Make 142 prairie points from 4½″ squares, and join to quilt edge.

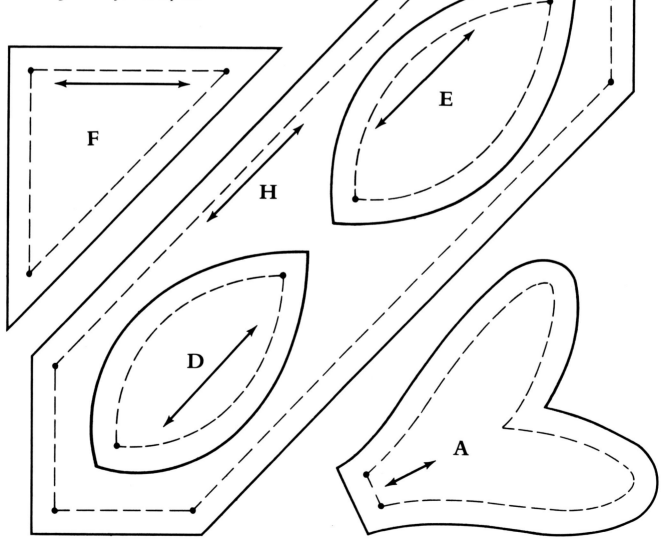

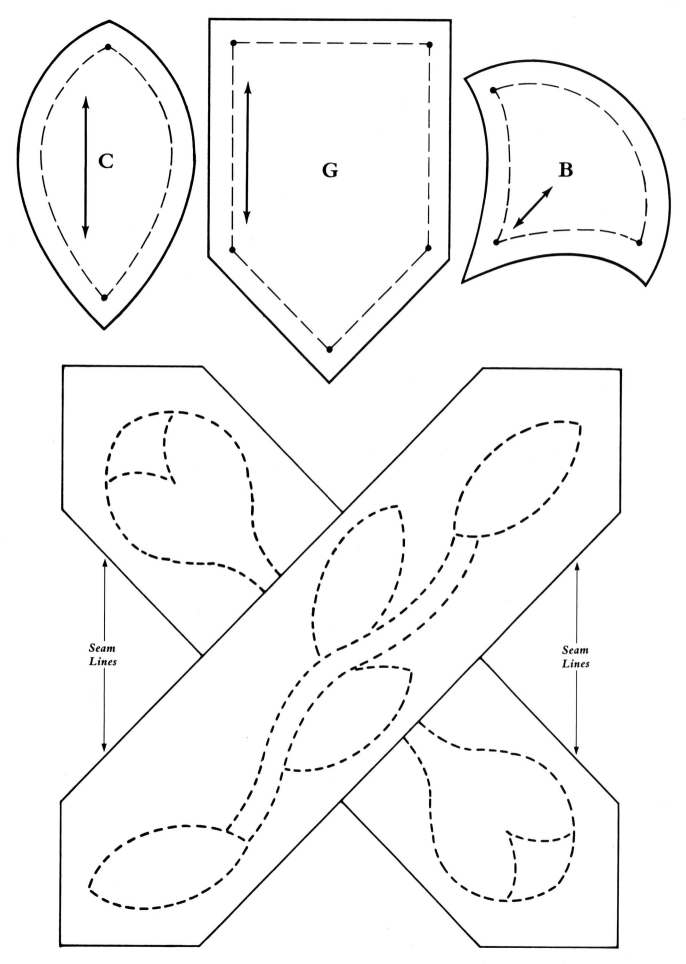

C

G

B

*Seam
Lines*

*Seam
Lines*

Odd Fellows March
1982

Odd Fellows March is a perfect example of Bobbie's style of quilting. It is a combination of her love for Amish colors, small pattern pieces, traditional block variations, and fine, embellished quilting. After choosing the Odd Fellows block, she graphed her design, established her borders, and then played with color placement. The result is this stunning array of blue and purple, set in a contrasting cream print with flecks of blue. The Odd Fellows block (sometimes known as Odd Fellows Chain) is pieced in alternating blue and purple combinations. Wide blue borders provide the perfect showcase for the Amish quilting pattern that was given to Bobbie by an Amish lady living in New York State. A final blue-and-purple sawtooth border encloses the quilt and complements the goose-chase border.

Bobbie Fuhrmann
Lancaster, New York

Patience should be Bobbie Fuhrmann's middle name! Her intricate, small-pieced quilts are all hand-pieced. (Some have taken as long as 2½ years just to complete the top.) One quilt top may contain anywhere from 6,000 to 7,500 pieces, but to Bobbie, the expectation is half the fun. "It's like a puzzle, and when you're done, everything has to fit together to make a successful piece," explains Bobbie. She likes to make her own adaptations of traditional patterns. Her designs evolve through a series of sketches, proceeding through exact graphed renditions. With so many pieces, the design stage is very important to Bobbie. "That's a lot of pieces to cut out, and then find that the proportions are wrong!" Professionally, she considers herself a fiber artist, since she is also an accomplished weaver and lace maker. But her primary love will always be quilting.

Odd Fellows March

Finished Quilt Size
95" x 95"

Number of Blocks and Finished Size
25 Odd Fellows
blocks—12" x 12" each

Fabric Requirements
Royal blue — 5¼ yd.
Purple for piecing
   and binding — 4½ yd.
Background — 4¾ yd.
Backing — 9 yd.

Number to Cut
Template A — 842 royal blue
736 background
246 purple
Template B — 128 purple
72 royal blue
Template C — 300 background
Template D — 25 background
Template E — 300 background
168 royal blue

Template F — 16 royal blue
Template G — 16 background
Template H — 16 background

Quilt Top Assembly
1. Piece 9 "blue" blocks, using blue and background pieces only. Piece 16 "purple" blocks, using purple triangles (B) instead of blue, and assemble as before. (See Odd Fellows March Piecing Diagram.)
2. Join blocks into rows as follows: 2 rows of 5 purple blocks, and 3 rows of 3 blue blocks flanked by purple blocks.
3. Join rows with purple block rows at the top and bottom, and the remaining 3 rows in the middle.
4. Cut 4 border strips from background fabric, 2" x 64", join to center section, and miter the corners.
5. Cut 4 purple border strips, 1¼" x 65", join to quilt, and miter the corners.
6. Piece goose-chase border and 4 corner sections. (See Goose-Chase Border Piecing Diagram.) Join the

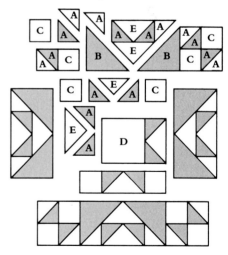

Odd Fellows March Piecing Diagram

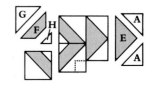

Goose-Chase Border Piecing Diagram

59

corner sections to the ends of two strips. Join strips to quilt top, placing corner block under corner of purple border and appliquéing purple border strip down onto corner block.

7. Cut 4 purple border strips, 1¼" wide, join to quilt, and miter the corners.

8. Cut 4 blue border strips, 9½" wide, join to quilt, and miter the corners.

9. Piece sawtooth border and join to quilt.

10. Cut 4 purple border strips, 1¼" wide, join to quilt, and miter the corners.

Quilting

Each 12" block is quilted with Bobbie's floral design. The background strip framing the blocks is quilted with a 1" diamond pattern. Quilt parallel lines, ¼" apart lengthwise, along purple border strips. Quilt outside seam line edge of purple strips. Quilt ¼" inside seam lines of goose-chase border. (See Quilting Diagram.) The Amish fleur-de-lis pattern is quilted along the 9" blue

border. To complete fleur-de-lis pattern, flip quilting template over so that long sides of pattern are set side by side and ½" apart. Place the next fleur-de-lis with its base set on the opposite edge of the blue border. Continue alternating fleur-de-lis positions around the blue border. Quilt ¼" inside seam line of purple triangles of sawtooth border, carrying lines to ⅜" of outside edge. Quilt inside seam line edge of blue triangles of sawtooth border.

Finished Edges
Bind with purple fabric.

Quilting Diagram

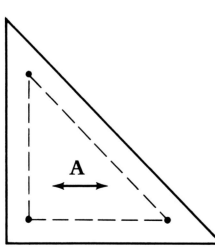

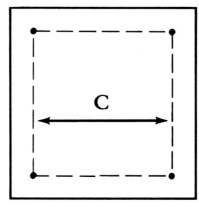

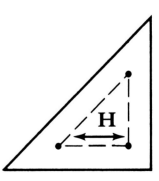

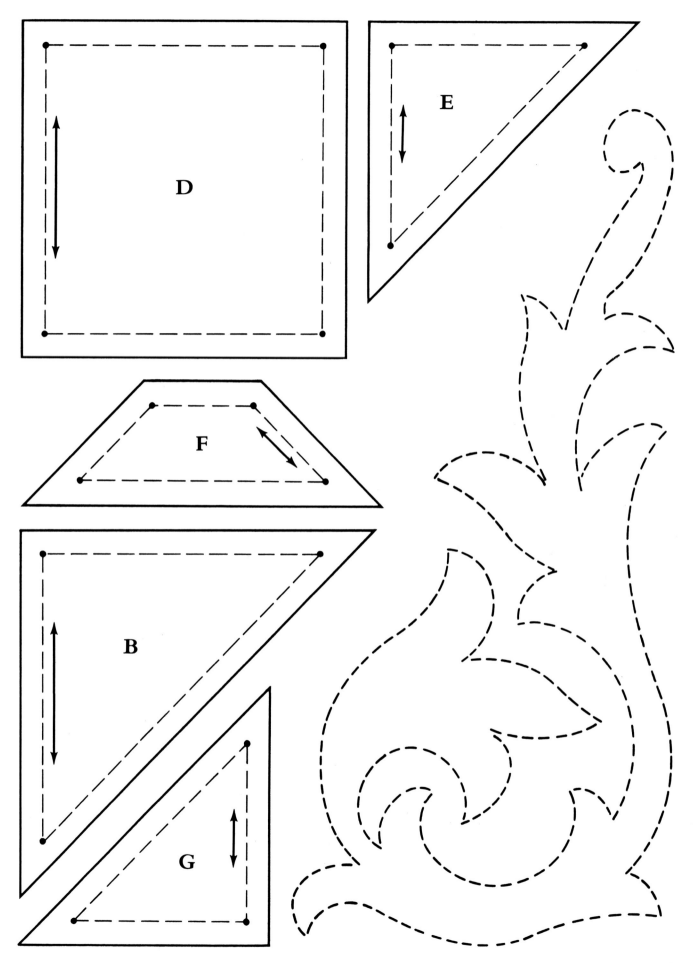

D

E

F

B

G

Queen's Petticoat
1983

It was love at first sight when Bobbie saw the Queen's Petticoat block in an issue of *Needlecraft for Today* (see our Resource Section). After reducing the pattern, she concentrated on surrounding the blocks with a series of borders that had great movement, complemented the central pattern, and framed it. Color and fabric choices were made using the same criteria, so that four pieced borders would dance around the center. You probably recognize the Windmill block in one, and the simple nine-patch square, set diagonally, in another. There's plenty of quilting too, used to emphasize certain areas and add new geometric shapes. Bobbie made the quilt for herself, and for the sheer joy and experience of making it!

Queen's Petticoat

Finished Quilt Size
82″ x 94″

Number of Blocks and Finished Size
80 Queen's Petticoat
  blocks—6″ x 6″ each
52 Windmill blocks—6″ x 6″ each

Fabric Requirements

Navy	—6½ yd.
Cream	—1½ yd.
Brown print	—3½ yd.
Dark red print	—3 yd.
Maroon floral stripe	—1¼ yd.
Red/cream print	— ½ yd.
Maroon print	— ¾ yd.
Red polka dot	— ¾ yd.
Cream/rust print I	— ½ yd.
Cream/rust print II	— ⅝ yd.
Navy floral stripe	—1¼ yd.
Backing fabric	—5½ yd.

Number to Cut

Template A	—160 navy
	138 cream
	138 brown print
	480 maroon floral stripe
	320 red/cream print
Template B	—568 navy
	160 brown print
	12 maroon floral stripe
	4 maroon print

Template C — 160 navy
480 cream
320 red print
Template D — 50 maroon floral
stripe
54 maroon print
Template E — 310 red polka dot
248 cream/rust
print I
Template F — 208 red print
Template G — 208 cream/rust
print II
208 navy floral
stripe

Quilt Top Assembly

1. Using templates A, B, and C, piece 80 Queen's Petticoat blocks. (See Queen's Petticoat Piecing Diagram.) Join 4 Queen's Petticoat blocks, rotating each 45° to make 1 large block. (See Queen's Petticoat Block Setting Diagram.) Make 20. Join large blocks into 5 rows of 4 blocks. Join rows.

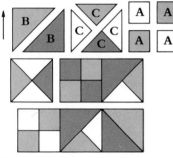

Queen's Petticoat Piecing Diagram

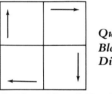

Queen's Petticoat Block Setting Diagram

2. First Pieced Border: Alternate maroon floral stripe and maroon print triangles (D) to make first border. Use 3 triangles (B) for corner piecing.
3. Second Pieced Border: Piece 5 polka dot squares (E) with 4 cream/rust print I squares (E) to form checkerboard block of second border. Make 62 blocks. Alternate blocks with navy triangles (B), and join to quilt. Thirteen blocks should fit nicely on top and bottom, 16 along the sides, and 4 corner blocks.
4. Third Pieced Border: Cut 4 border strips the length of quilt sides and 4 border strips for top and bottom from brown print, 1½" wide. Cut 1½" squares from brown print

and cream. Alternate colors and join to form a strip. Make strips for sides, top, and bottom. Piece 1 strip between 2 brown print border strips. Make 4. Join to quilt. (Finished third border width = 3".)
5. Windmill Border: Using triangles F and G, piece 52 Windmill blocks. (See Windmill Block Piecing Diagram.) Join blocks into border strips (11 for top and bottom, 13 along the sides, and 4 corner blocks), and join to quilt.

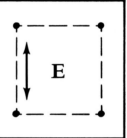

Windmill Block Piecing Diagram

6. Cut 2" navy border strips, join to quilt, and miter corners.

Quilting
Refer to Quilting Diagram for Queen's Petticoat block. Quilt ¼" inside seam lines of triangles for first border. Quilt ¼" inside seam lines of checkerboard block, and 3 horizontal parallel lines ⅜" apart in each navy triangle. Quilt ¼" inside outer seam lines of brown strips, and inside seam lines of second border squares. Quilt ¼" inside seam lines of Windmill block. Duplicate triangle shape ½" inside first quilting line of large Windmill block triangles (F). Quilt ¼" inside seam line of navy border strip.

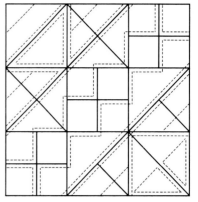

Quilting Diagram

Finished Edges
Bind with navy fabric.

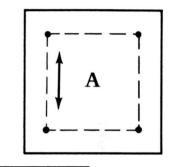

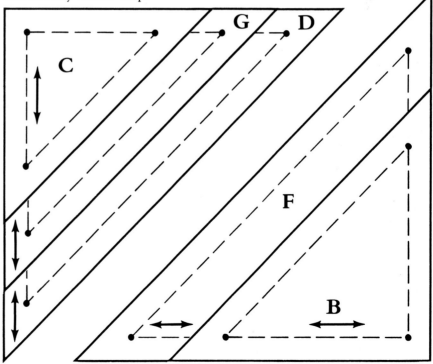

Flavin Glover
Auburn, Alabama

Hemlocks
1985

Bring the majestic, serene spirit of a thicket of hemlocks into your home with Flavin's quilted wall hanging. This quilted forest is totally created from Rail Fence blocks, pieced in muted shades of greens, creams, and browns. Flavin continuously challenges herself to take traditional, perpendicular blocks, such as Rail Fence, and manipulate them into pictorial and/or scenic quilts. Says Flavin, "This design resulted from looking at the Rail Fence pattern as a grid in which to find new shapes, and from a fondness for trees and forests."

Finished Quilt Size
56″ x 62″

Number of Blocks and Finished Size
255 Rail Fence blocks—3″ x 3″ each

Fabric Requirements
Assorted dk. greens — 1½ yd. total
Assorted browns   — ½ yd. total
Assorted lt. greens — 1¼ yd. total
Assorted creams   — 2 yd. total
Dk. green
    for borders   — 1¾ yd.
Brown for borders
    and binding   — 3 yd.
Backing fabric   — 3¾ yd.

Number to Cut
Rail Fence template — 393 dk.
                      greens
                      79 browns
                      190 lt.
                      greens
                      432 creams

Flavin made many independent efforts to learn to quilt. Her mother, also a quilter, observed her efforts and declared that Flavin would never be much of a quilter. "Each time I sought Mom's help, she wisely declined," Flavin told us. "Of course, this drove my determination higher!" One Christmas when Flavin came home from college, her mother mentioned to her, "Flav, I have a quilt in the frame I don't care much for, so you can help me quilt it." Flavin responded, "Gee thanks, Mom, for all the encouragement!" Nonetheless, Flavin proceeded to quilt it. "That chance was the best Christmas gift she could have given me. We still laugh about it today," recalls Flavin, whose list of quilting awards and exhibits has gained the admiration of many.

Flavin, a full-time recreational therapist, feels a great drive to quilt. "I pursue quilting with more vigor and determination than any other endeavor. Quilting is my vehicle to express creativity and to make my own way. In somewhat of a contradiction though, it also evokes warmth, security, and tradition. On both sides I see continuity, in that quilting gives me a handle on my future."

Here, Flavin is sharing her Rail Fence block design of *Hemlocks,* but be sure to turn to "Log Cabin Turnaround" to examine Flavin's splendid *Row Houses* quilt.

Quilt Top Assembly

1. Join 4 rails to make one Rail Fence block. Make blocks according to chart below.

2. Join rail fence blocks into rows of 15, using diagram for placement. Join rows.

3. Cut 4 border strips of brown fabric, 1½″ wide, and join to Rail Fence blocks.

4. Cut 4 border strips of green fabric, 1¼″ wide, and join to quilt.

5. Cut 4 border strips of brown fabric, 1½″ wide, and join to quilt.

6. The fourth border is made of rail pieces in greens and creams, joined end to end. 74 rails are used: 18 across the width and 19 along the length. Flavin arranged rails so that the rails went from the darkest greens at the bottom to lighter greens and creams on the sides and top.

7. Cut brown fabric for last border strips 2½″ wide, and join to quilt.

Quilting

Refer to Quilting Diagram, mark quilting lines on trees, and quilt. Outline-quilt outside seam lines of tree trunks, background, and borders.

Block Rail Colors	Number to Make
4 dark greens	57
3 dark greens and 1 cream on end	20
3 dark greens and 1 cream in middle	3
2 dark greens in middle and 2 creams	12
2 dark greens and 2 creams together	15
4 browns	13
2 dark browns in middle and 2 creams	12
1 dark brown on end and 3 creams	2
4 light greens	25
3 light greens and 1 cream on end	20
2 light greens in middle and 2 creams	8
4 creams	59
3 creams and 1 light green on end	1
2 creams and 2 light greens together	5
1 dark green, cream, and 2 light greens together	1
2 dark greens together, cream, and 1 light green	1
2 dark greens together, cream, and 1 dark brown	1

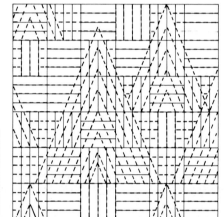

Quilting Diagram

Finished Edges

Bind with brown fabric.

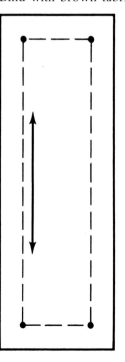

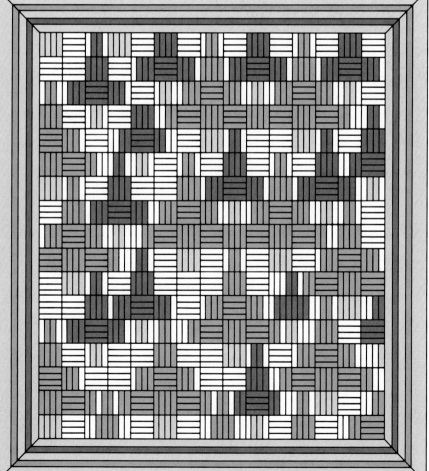

65

Patti Connor

Collinsville, Illinois

The Big Black Quilt
1986

Here's Patti's first bed-size quilt, *The Big Black Quilt*. "I had so many ideas of what to make for my first bed-size quilt that I was having a lot of trouble getting started. I couldn't focus on any one idea," says Patti.

With a little bit of mathematical help from her husband, Chuck, *The Big Black Quilt* became a reality. It is a combination of the Carolina Lily block surrounded by Buttercup blocks, pieced in a multitude of shades of blues, purples, and reds. (Patti was inspired by Mary Ellen Hopkins's Buttercup block. See Resource Section for details.) All of this is contrasted on a field of black, which is machine-quilted as well as hand-quilted. Quilting designs for corner triangles are Patti's originals. And what does Patti think about *The Big Black Quilt*? "I wanted to make a strong graphic statement, and I think I did!"

At 30 years of age, Patti Connor was a successful artist with lots of influence and responsibility, and all the perks and salary she could want. But she was looking for something more. She was encouraged to try quilting by a local quilt guild member, bought several books on quilting, and tried her hand at it. "I was hooked!" exclaims Patti.

That was only a year and a half ago. Today, she has begun a small business called A Quilt of a Different Color, and has completed three wall hangings, one full-size quilt, and some quilted clothing. Her artistic background plays a major role in her quilt designs. Every detail for each quilt is worked out on paper before she cuts a piece of fabric. "I'm very used to playing and sketching and dreaming, something others often feel is wasting time, but for me is essential to good design," Patti explains.

Turn to "Log Cabin Turnaround" to see Patti's first experiment with Log Cabin blocks for a Christmas wall hanging.

The Big Black Quilt

Finished Quilt Size
93″ x 118″

Number of Blocks and Finished Size
1 Carolina Lily
   block—30½″ x 30½″
32 Buttercup blocks—12″ x 12″ each

Fabric Requirements
Black	—5½ yd.
Red	—1¾ yd.
Green	—1¼ yd.
Wine	—2 yd.
Teal	—1 yd.
Blue	—1 yd.
Light blue	— ¼ yd.
Blue-violet	—2 yd.
Light blue-violet	— ¼ yd.
Light wine	— ¼ yd.
Binding	—1¼ yd.
Backing	—9 yd.

Number to Cut

Template A — 96 black
8 wine
4 teal
4 blue
4 light blue
4 blue-violet
4 light blue-violet
4 light wine

Template B — 64 green
16 wine
8 teal
8 blue
8 light blue
8 blue-violet
8 light blue-violet
8 light wine
128 black

Template C — 28 red
Template D — 28 black
Template E — 28 black
Template F — 3 black
Template G — 1 black
Template H — 12 red
Template I — 2 green
Template J — 6 black
Template K — 1 black
3 green
Template L — 1 black
Template M — 2 black
Right triangles — 24 black, 12″
on sides, add ¼″ seam allowance;
4 red, 24⅜″ on sides, add ¼″ seam
allowance

Quilt Top Assembly

1. To piece Carolina Lily block,
join 4 red diamonds (H) to make
each lily. (See Lily Block Piecing
Diagram I.) Make 3 lilies. Set in
black squares (F) and triangles (J)
between points of lilies. Attach

*Lily Block
Piecing
Diagram I*

green triangles (K) to form base of
lilies. Join each large black triangle
(M) to the sides of one of the lilies
to form top section. Hand-appliqué
the curved stem to the large black
rectangle (G). Attach the remaining
2 lilies to either side of the rectangle, to complete middle section. For
bottom section, sew one leaf (I) to
each side of black triangle K, and
sew triangle L to the bottom. Join
the bottom section to the middle
section, and hand-appliqué the
straight stem in place. (See Lily
Block Piecing Diagram II.) Sew the
top section to the rest of the block.

2. Cut 4 black strips, 1¼″ wide,
join to the Lily block, and miter
the corners. Cut 4 teal strips, 2″
wide, join to the Lily block, and
miter the corners.

*Lily Block
Piecing
Diagram II*

3. For Buttercup blocks, piece all
small red squares (C) to small black
rectangles (D). Join all these units
to the black rectangles (E). (See
Buttercup Block Piecing Diagram.)

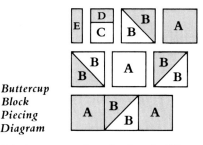

*Buttercup
Block
Piecing
Diagram*

Stitch every colored triangle (B)
(including green) to a black triangle
(B). Lay out a block at a time; sew
the patches into rows and the rows
into blocks. Make 28 Buttercup
blocks, making 4 blocks of each of
the 7 colors.

4. Following Quilt Diagram, sew
Buttercup blocks and 12″ black
right triangles into rows for each
quarter of the quilt. Sew the rows
together, matching seam lines. Cut
4 wine strips, 2″ wide, and join to
each outside edge of Buttercup
quarter section. Cut 4 blue-violet
strips, 3″ wide, and join to each
outside edge of Buttercup quarter
section. Join Buttercup quarter sections to Lily block and quarters together along their adjoining edges.

5. For corner sections, cut 8 blue
strips, 1½″ wide. (See Quilt Top
Assembly Diagram.) Join a strip to
perpendicular sides of each 24⅜″
red right triangle, and miter corner.
Using wine color, piece 1 Buttercup block for each corner, omitting
the center bud pieces. Piece into 3
rows as before, but join only the
middle row to the bottom row. Set
top row aside.

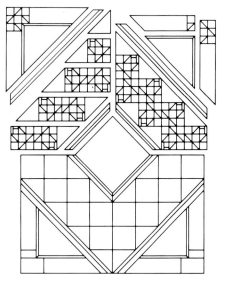

Quilt Top Assembly Diagram

6. Cut 8 black border strips, 8½″
wide, to run along perpendicular
sides of corner triangles. Join a
black border strip to the side of
two-row Buttercup block. (See
Quilt Top Assembly Diagram.)
Join a black border strip to the top
of the single-row Buttercup block.
Join these sections lengthwise to the
sides of the corner triangle. Repeat
for all 4 corners. Trim blue and
black borders to a 45° angle, even
with hypotenuse of corner triangles.
Attach corner sections to quilt.

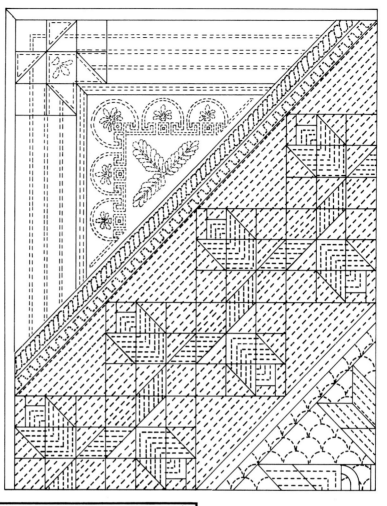

Quilting

Refer to Quilting Diagram for placement of quilting patterns. Parallel lines within lily and buttercup pieces are ¾″ apart. Parallel lines 1″ apart are machine-quilted in large black areas surrounding Buttercup blocks. If you want to schedule your time, Patti tells us that lots of wrestling is involved, so machine-quilting time is about 3 hours per quarter. Outer black borders are also machine-quilted in 3 sets of parallel lines, ¼″ apart, but not until hand quilting on red triangles is completed. Feathering on red triangles is centered and quilted on triangle's hypotenuse. Patti used black quilting thread throughout.

Finished Edges

Bind with 5½″-wide teal bias strips. Fold in half lengthwise and press carefully. Right sides together and raw edges even with the quilt top, stitch in place. Fold around to back, miter corners, and blind-stitch in place.

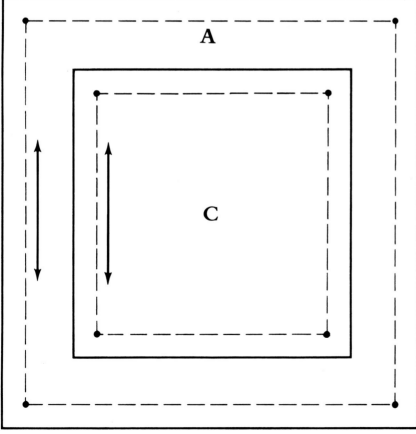

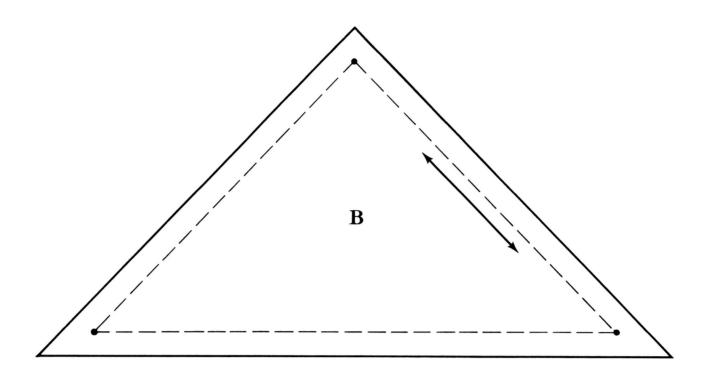

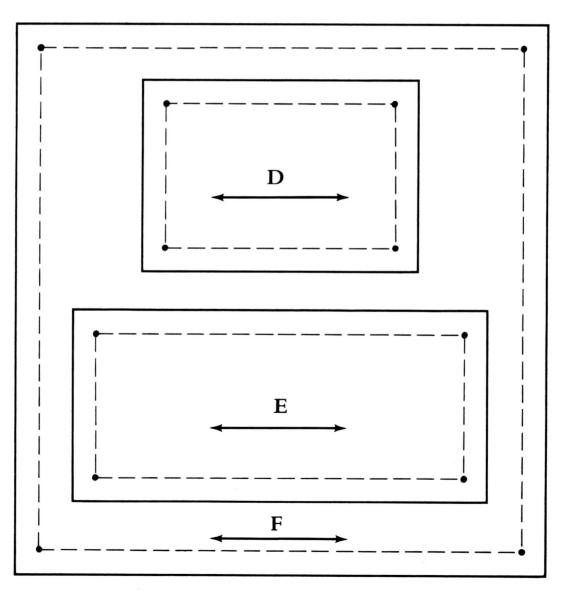

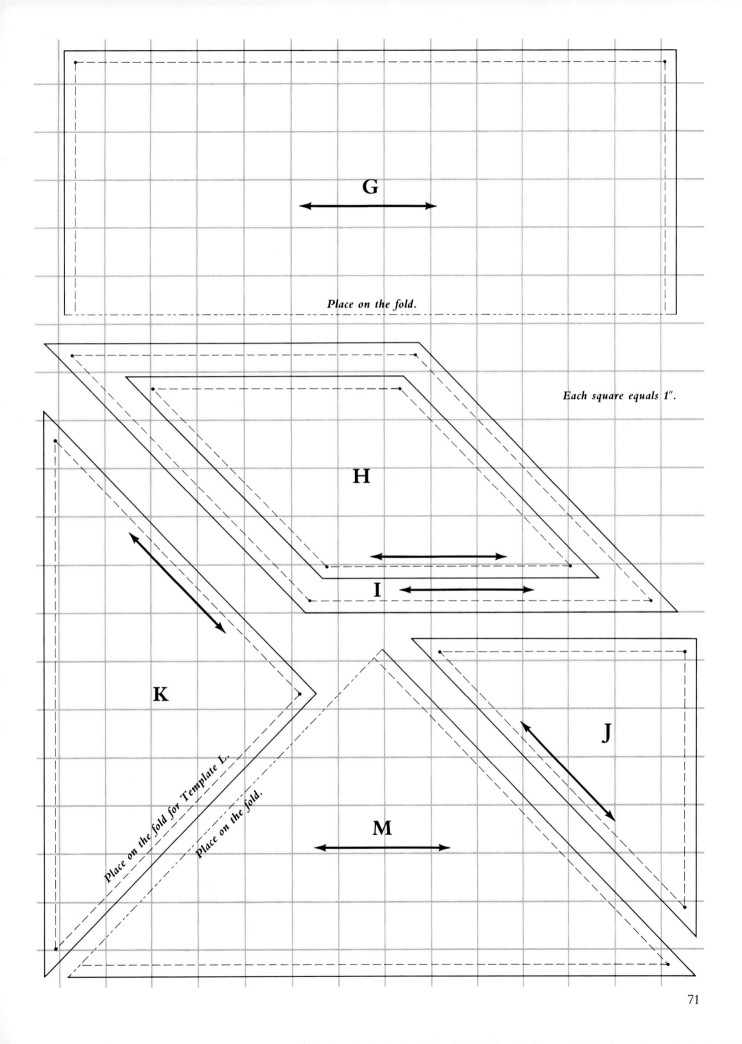

G

H

I

K

J

M

Place on the fold.

Each square equals 1".

Place on the fold for Template L.

Place on the fold.

Judy Wasserman Hearst

Milwaukee, Wisconsin

A dedicated weaver and fiber artist for many years, Judy's devotion to quilting is a fairly recent development in her busy life as professional quilter, teacher, wife, and mother. After taking a class in contemporary quilting some six years ago, Judy focused her attention on quilting and its use as an art medium. "Quilting is important to so many people's lives, and my commitment to quilting extends further than the needle and thread," says Judy. "I am an active member of quilt guilds, and as an artist, I am always promoting quilting as a medium in which an artist can create."

Teaching and lecturing, Judy encourages women to create designs and patterns unique to our times, to perpetuate the folk art of quilting. Since quilts are no longer considered survival items, Judy explains, "If quilting is to flourish into the future, it may be through its use as an art medium. As the practical need has diminished, creative expression has taken on more significance." For Judy, contemporary quilts link the past to the present and on into the future.

Color Study
1986

Color Study is just that—a study of warm, hot, and cool fabric colors interlocked with strips of white polished cotton, with just enough quilting to give it texture. Assembled in a wall-hanging format with no pattern pieces, it is quick and easy to make. Here's your chance to put into practice everything you learned in that last color workshop you attended. Here's your chance to put all those scraps to good use, to experiment, to go crazy with color, and try that color combination you never had the nerve to try on "Aunt Mary's" quilt.

As Judy says, *Color Study* is creative play in a structured manner." Don't be surprised to hear yourself saying—I like that! Look what's happening here! Those are the colors I want to use on my next quilt!—And no one would be happier to hear you say those things than Judy.

If you prefer to buy the fabric, pick out several bolts and lay them side by side to see what happens with the colors before you buy. You'll discover a hot color may "go warm" next to a cool color, and so on, and so on. . . . Otherwise, just dig into your scrap bag and have some fun!

Color Study

Finished Quilt Size
Approximately 40″ x 52″

Fabric Requirements
White polished
  cotton   — 1 yd.
Assorted fabrics
  for strip piecing — 1½ yd. total
  (warms, hots, and cools)
Backing   — 2 yd.
Striped fabric
  for binding   — ½ yd.

Quilt Top Assembly
1. Cut the following strips from white and group by widths:
2½″ wide   — 4 strips
2″ wide   — 4 strips
1½″ wide   — 4 strips
1¼″ wide   — 3 strips

One extra white strip any width to add to color bands
2. Cut crosswise of grain 36 to 40 strips of the assorted fabric in widths from 3″ to 5″. Judy suggests cutting more warm and hot colors because you will need more of these strips.
3. Randomly sew strips of warm colors together into groups of 3 to 5 in any combination. Here is where you can have some fun. Judy says to try some unusual combinations for extra visual impact. Experiment!! Use creative play and

intuition instead of color coordination in arrangement of colors. Judy recommends pressing seams of the strip piece all in one direction on the wrong side first, and then on the right side.
4. Repeat step 3 with cool colors. Remember, experiment with your color combinations.
5. Cut widths of the strip piece as shown in the table below, perpendicular to sewn strips. Group by widths. Cut enough strips to make 40″ rows.

Fabric Color	3½″ wide	3″ wide	2½″ wide	2″ wide
Warms and Hots	3—40″ rows	2—40″ rows	2—40″ rows	3—40″ rows
Cools			4—40″ rows	2—40″ rows

6. Sew strips of equal widths together randomly. Change direction of fabric to get as much variety as possible. Cut and add small amounts of white or small unexpected opposite hues. Rearrange! Rearrange! as much as desired. Make 16 rows as shown in table.

7. Sew strips and pieced rows together lengthwise, stitching seams in opposite directions to keep pieced top even. Alternate pieced rows with white strips in the following order: 3½″ warm, 2½″ white, 3″ cool, 2″ white, 2½″ warm, 1½″ white, 3″ cool, 1½″ white, 2″ warm, 1¼″ white, 2″ cool, 2″ white, 2″ hot, 2½″ white, 3″ hot, and 1¼″ white. This is the center. Repeat backwards from here, omitting the 1¼″ white strip. Judy uses a medium gray thread throughout and sets her machine stitch length at a small setting of 10 to 12 stitches per inch.

Quilting
Fill the white strips with ¼″ parallel lines of quilting. Judy suggests using ¼″ masking tape as a guide.

Finished Edges
Bind with 3″ binding made from the striped fabric. Attach a casing of matching fabric to the back for hanging.

73

Liz Porter

Lorimor, Iowa

Marianne Fons

Winterset, Iowa

Liz and Marianne are pictured here with Helen Martens (center), who did the beautiful quilting on Tulip Vine.

Tulip Vine
1984

Toss 48 brightly colored tulips around oval vines, and a simple tulip pattern becomes this spectacular field of movement and symmetry. Marianne and Liz designed this stylized tulip pattern that is simple and easy to appliqué. It readily lends itself to other color interpretations and is equally suited to a traditional as well as contemporary mode.

If you want to learn to quilt, just go to your local college extension center and demand that they teach a class! That's exactly what Marianne Fons did, and it led to her successful, ten-year, quilt-designing relationship with Liz Porter. Another offspring of her initiative was the formation of the Heritage Quilters of Winterset, Iowa, which is still active today.

After an initial period of team teaching, Marianne and Liz began to express their artistic inclinations in the *designing* of quilts. Their designs range from original to interpretations of traditional patterns. As Marianne and Liz told us, they may use an old design in a new way or a new design in a traditional way, but would never copy a quilt exactly.

Quilting has offered them a chance to travel the United States and meet scores of quilters, and to participate in an activity that is fun and rewarding. "Quilting lasts, and I can see my day's accomplishment even if it is just a few stitches," says Liz.

To the delight of these mothers, quilting has allowed them the joy of exploring their creative cravings at home while raising their families. "I never really have to stop work to prepare meals," explains Marianne. "I can start the stew and go back in my studio and work, stopping to stir every so often." For our benefit, let's hope they never stop quilting and stirring.

Tulip Vine

Finished Quilt Size
Approximately 98" x 82"

Fabric Requirements
Unbleached muslin	—6 yd. for quilt top 6 yd. for backing
Solid dark green	—2½ yd.
Solid red	— ⅝ yd.
Red print	—1 yd.

Number to Cut
Tulips	—24 solid red 46 red print
Tulip tips	—46 solid red 24 red print
Leaves	—120 dark green

Quilt Top Assembly
1. Make a master placement oval pattern on an 18" x 20" piece of paper, by using the quarter oval given. Use the tulip and leaf templates to draw placement lines on master pattern. Draw perpendicular lines to indicate center of pattern. (See Placement Diagram.) Darken lines on front and back of paper pattern.

Placement Diagram

2. From unbleached muslin, cut 3 panels, 20½" x 108", and 2 border panels, 11½" x 108". Do not cut scallops at this time. Fold muslin panel in half twice, and finger-crease to find center. Place the muslin panel over the master placement pattern, aligning the center lines of the placement pattern with the center of the panel. Mark placement lines on the muslin. Start at the center of the panel, and repeat pattern five times on each panel. Flip the placement pattern to reverse the design for every other oval. Do this for the three quilt-top panels.

3. From dark green fabric, cut 60 bias strips, 8" long and 1¼" wide, for vines. Marianne and Liz recommend not using continuous bias, because the vines are prettier without seams. Press strips into thirds lengthwise. Make sure the underneath raw edge is hidden by a top fold. Baste strips along placement lines, using the marked line as the *inner* curve of the vine.

4. Pin or baste leaves and tulips in position, combining solid tips with print tulips and print tips with solid tulips. Hand-appliqué vines, tulips, and leaves. Begin with the inner edge of the vine to keep bias smooth.

5. Sew the three panels together with a ¼" seam. Add border panels to each side.

6. Mark quilt edges for scallops, using scallop template. *Do not cut scallops until quilting is completed.*

7. Using tulip templates, mark placement lines for tulips 1½" from each scallop peak.

8. Hand-appliqué print tulips with solid red tips, to complete border design.

Quilting

Quilt Design I in the center of each tulip vine oval. Quilt Design II on border scallops. (Remember only one-half of the quilting pattern is given since the patterns are symmetrical.) Quilt a 1" diagonal square grid on remaining areas.

Finished Edges

Using scallop guideline, trim quilt edges. Bind edges with folded 2" wide, French-folded bias binding in dark green fabric.

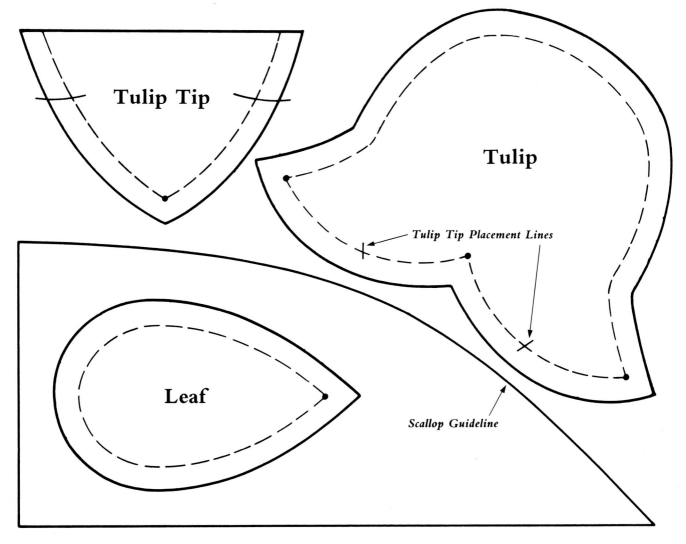

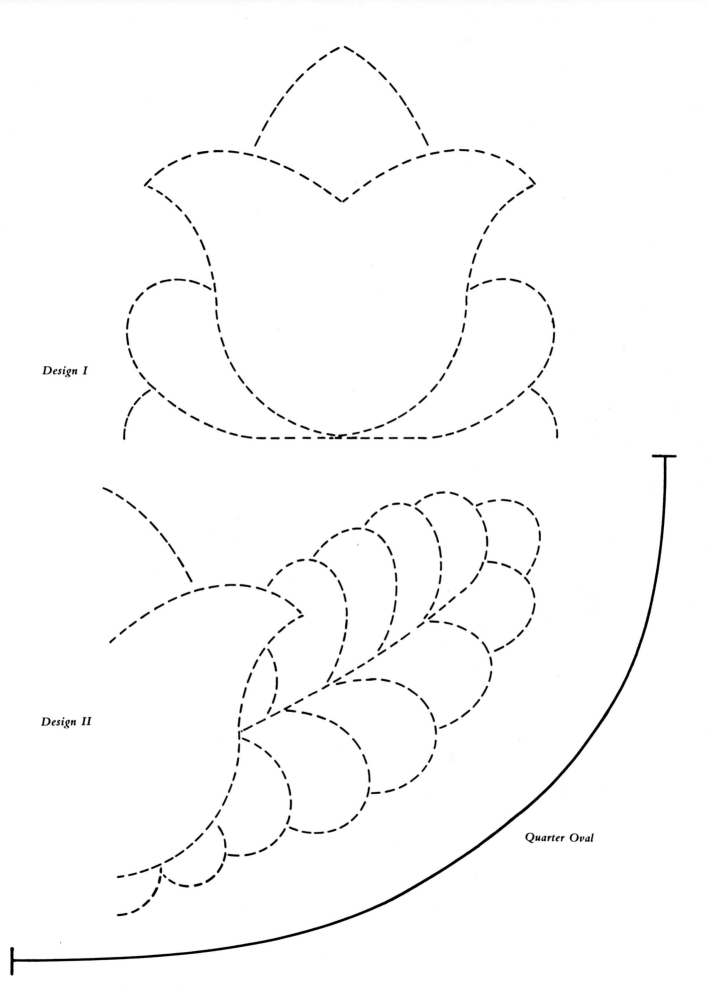

Design I

Design II

Quarter Oval

77

Ray Jansen
Omaha, Nebraska

In between fighting fires as a full-time fireman, Ray began quilting as a hobby, because he wanted to use quilt tops as an art form. Having taken several art courses in high school and elsewhere, the quilting medium gave Ray the opportunity to illustrate his color-design talents in fabric. Each of his quilts demonstrates a wide variety of color-plays with geometric shapes.

Ray is a member of the Omaha Quilters Guild, and most of his quilts are given away to friends and family as gifts. For Ray, a self-taught quilter, machine piecing and machine quilting are the only way to go! After eight quilts in six years, Ray says, "I'm still learning."

Christmas Quilt

Finished Quilt Size
93" x 108"

Fabric Requirements
White — 4½ yd.
Assorted
  Christmas fabrics — ¼ yd. each
(Please note: ¼ yd. will make 42 squares. *Largest* number used per bargello row is 35.)
White for backing
  and binding — 9 yd.

Number to Cut
Square — 607 white
898 assorted
Christmas fabrics

Quilt Top Assembly
1. Join 43 squares into vertical rows to form bargello pattern, as shown in quilt photograph. Each row begins and ends with a white square. Make 35 rows. Join rows.
2. Cut 2 border strips from white, 3" wide, and join to sides of quilt.

3. Cut backing large enough to finish edges with a rolled hem.

Machine Quilting
Fold quilt top in half lengthwise along a seam line, center it on batting and backing, and pin along seam line. Machine-quilt in-the-ditch of this lengthwise seam. Remove pins and repeat for next seam from the center, until all lengthwise seams have been machine-quilted.

Finished Edges
Ray trimmed bottom corners at a 45° angle to prevent quilt from touching the floor when placed on a bed. Turn 1" of backing to quilt front, turn edge under ¼", and machine-stitch along binding edge.

Christmas Quilt
1985
This bargello-style quilt is a perfect
example of Ray's designing talents.
Two-inch squares of Christmas red
and green prints stair-step across
this quilt to create layers of Christmas joy. In-the-ditch machine quilting adds dimension and more time
to work on the next quilt.

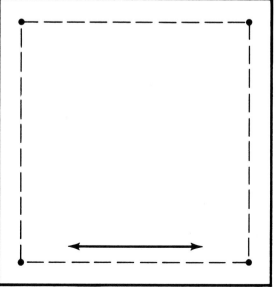

Katharine is basically a self-taught quilter. She learned one day while in bed with the flu and pregnant with her first son, Nicholas. "My husband bought me some fabric to keep me busy (and quiet)," explains Katharine. Since then, her sons have provided her with ample stimulation and inspiration for more than 30 quilts in four and a half years. She says, "Quilting is a way of expressing myself, of sorting out thoughts and emotions, of sifting through daily experiences, frustrations, and joys, to produce a visual, tactile record of a day, a month, a minute. It calms my nerves and soothes my soul. It is a way to wrap my children in love at night, to delight them during the day. Quilting has helped to draw me out of myself; it has given me self-confidence and helped me to see that I am a unique individual with a unique view of life."

Katharine R. Brainard
Takoma Park, Maryland

Cat Quilt II
1985
Cat Quilt II was born shortly after Katharine's second son, Alexander, was born. (There does seem to be a definite connection, at least in Katharine's life, between having sons and designing quilts.) Katharine made *Cat Quilt I* in 1982 shortly after the birth of her first son, Nicholas, to keep her "mind from turning to oatmeal"! *Cat Quilt I* was made with bright primary colors, while *Cat Quilt II* contains more subtle colors and prints and a lot more quilting. The quilt was inspired by their family cat, Botley, whom Katharine described as a rather silly cat that just sat and stared with saucer eyes. So Katharine invites you to capture your favorite kitty cat in quilt block format, hang it(him/her) on the wall, and one day you may find your cat staring at himself on the wall, instead of at you!

Cat Quilt II

Finished Quilt Size
40" x 40"

Number of Blocks and Finished Size
9 Cat blocks—10" x 10" each

Fabric Requirements
Blue print   —1 yd.
Cream/blue print   —1 yd.
Pink   — ⅛ yd.
Yellow   — ⅛ yd.
Green print   — ¾ yd.
Assorted pink prints   —1 yd. total
Pink print for backing —1¼ yd.

Embroidery Floss
5 skeins blue, 2 skeins pink

Number to Cut
Templates A–Q   —9 each from
(except G)   cream/blue print
Template F   —9 blue print
Template G   —18 blue print
        18 cream/blue
        print
Template I   —9 blue print
        9 green print
Template R   —18 blue print
Template S   —45 blue print
        18 yellow
Template T   —9 blue print
Template U   —18 blue print
Template V   —9 pink
Template W   —9 blue print
Templates X–Z   —9 each from
        blue print
Template AA   —18 blue print
Template BB   —18 pink
Template CC   —9 blue print
Template DD   —9 blue print
Template EE   —18 assorted
        pink prints

Quilt Top Assembly
1. Piece as shown into 4 sections (see Cat Block Piecing Diagram). Join. Make 9 cat blocks.

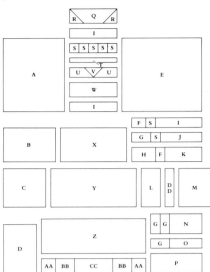

Cat Block Piecing Diagram

2. Embroider eyes, whiskers, and paws with 2 strands of blue in a daisy chain stitch. Embroider mouth in pink in same manner. (See Embroidery Diagram.)

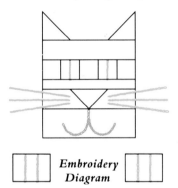

Embroidery Diagram

3. Appliqué 2 hearts to each block. Here is where Katharine used her pink prints, putting 2 different pink hearts in each block.

4. Cut 2 sashing strips, 1½" x 10½", and 2 sashing strips, 1½" x 12½", for each block from a pink print. (Katharine grouped her Cat blocks into 3s and used a different pink print for each group.) Join the shorter strips to top and bottom of each block, and the remaining strips to opposite sides of each block. Repeat for each block.

5. Cut 12 sashing strips for Cat blocks, 1" wide, from green print. Alternate 4 sashing strips with 3 Cat blocks and join, beginning with a sashing strip to form a row. Make 3 rows. Katharine set her Cat blocks so that a sashing strip of each pink print appears on each row in a different order.

6. Join 4 pink accent squares with ends of 3 green sashing strips in alternating fashion. Make 4 sashing strips.

7. Alternate Cat block rows with sashing strips and join, beginning with a sashing strip.

Quilting and Finished Edges
Cut backing 41" square, to allow for a rolled hem for finished edges. Quilt Cat block (this does not include the pink sashing) with a 1" crosshatch pattern.

  Turn ¾" of backing to the front, turn edge under ¼", and secure with a slipstitch. Katharine quilted a twisted rope pattern on all pink and green sashing, including the ½" rolled hem along the quilt edges. Attach a casing of matching fabric to back for hanging.

Blockhead

We couldn't resist letting you peek at Katharine's *Blockhead* quilt as well. All of you mothers with playful tykes who leave a trail of toys and blocks from room to room will enjoy and appreciate *Blockhead*. As Katharine told us, "This quilt was designed to express a moment's feeling one rainy afternoon when I had picked the children's blocks up off the floor for the umpteenth time. When I came back into the room and saw them on the floor *again,* I gave up and started playing with them. This quilt represents what I looked like and felt like at that moment."

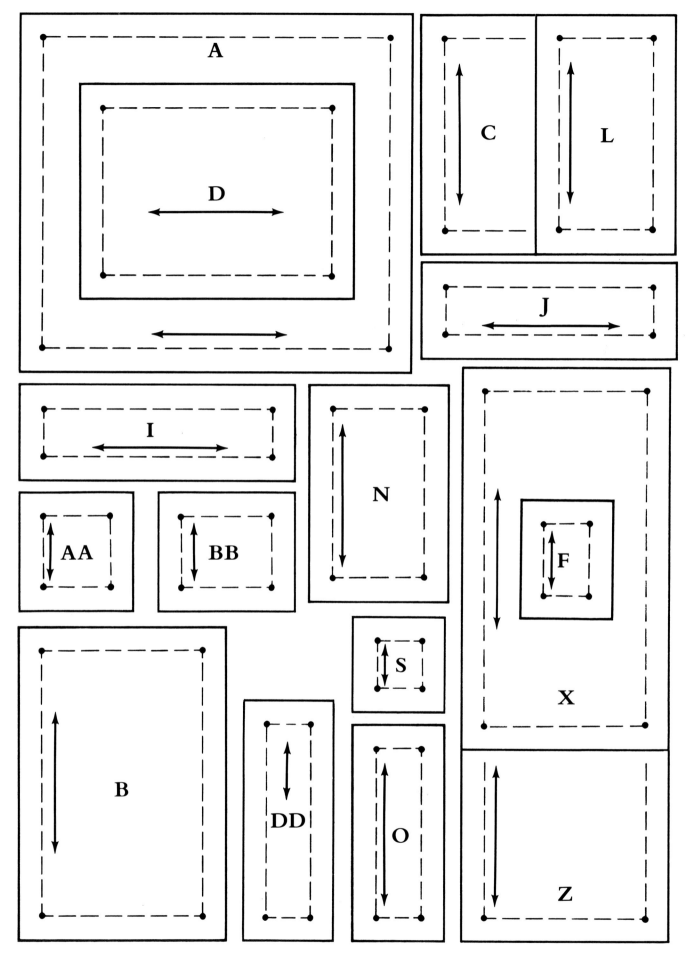

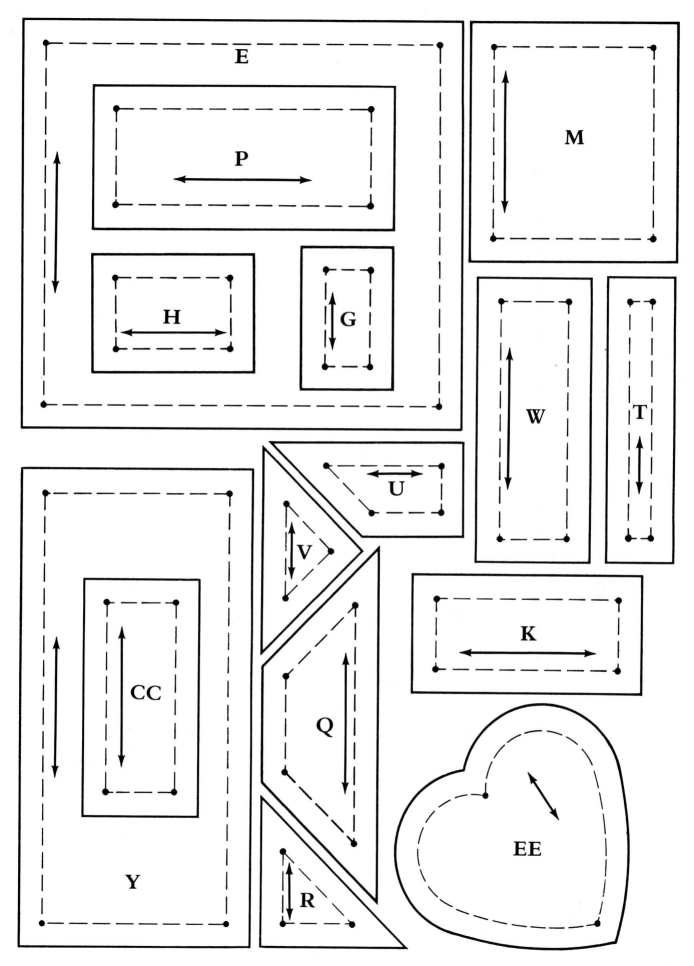

Charlotte Warr Andersen

Kearns, Utah

Charlotte credits quilting with giving her an identity beyond being a housewife and mother, and an outlet for her artistic skills. As Charlotte told us, "It has given me more purpose in life." In three short years of quilting, Charlotte has already achieved national recognition for her quilting endeavors, as the second place winner of The Great American Quilt Contest, held in celebration of the Statue of Liberty Centennial. As secretary of the Utah Quilt Guild, she finds great joy in being able to associate with other quilters and in promoting quilting in general.

Most of Charlotte's quilts are original designs or elaborations of traditional patterns, as you will see with the *Seven Sisters Medallion* below. In addition, please be sure to feast your eyes on one of her original wall hangings, *Upstream*, which is featured in our "Designer Gallery."

Charlotte's inspiration for her quilts comes from everywhere. "I look at something and see how it can be made into a quilt," says Charlotte. "Some of these ideas stick in my mind; most leave, but those that stick keep begging at me—'Make me, make me!'"

Seven Sisters Medallion
1985

Charlotte has always been charmed by the Seven Sisters pattern, but never liked the fact that if you wanted a rectangular quilt, the outside hexagons would be cut in half. Therefore, she "medallioned" it, and surrounded it with a series of pieced borders to add dimension and movement. Charlotte designed a stylized trefoil pattern for each large triangle, and extended parallel lines of quilting from the medallion to the borders to accentuate the medallion even more. This quilt received the 1985 Award of Excellence from the Springville Art Museum, Springville, Utah; and the Mountain Mist Best of Show award at the 1985 Utah State Fair.

Seven Sisters Medallion

Finished Quilt Size
96" x 88"

Fabric Requirements

Solid dark green	—1½ yd.
Solid red for piecing and binding	—2½ yd.
Dark green print	—1⅞ yd.
Cream print	—2¾ yd.
Solid cream	—7 yd.
Gold/green floral stripe	—1 yd.
Green/red floral stripe for first border	—2¼ yd.
Green/black floral stripe for third border	—2¾ yd.
Backing fabric	—8 yd.

Number to Cut

Template A	—36 dk green
	6 red
	126 dk green print
	126 cream print
	126 cream
Template B	—42 cream
Template C	—208 dk green
	208 red
Template D	—6 dk green
	6 red
Template E	—4 red
Template F	—48 cream
Template G	—208 cream
Template H	—208 cream print
Template I	—8 red
Template J	—32 cream

Quilt Top Assembly

1. Join sides of 6 diamonds (A) to form a star. Make 6 solid green stars, 18 green print stars, and 18 cream print stars. Piece Seven Sisters block using 3 cream print stars, 3 green print stars, and a solid green star in center. Make 6 blocks. Make 1 additional block with 3 green print stars, 3 cream print stars, and 1 red star in the center. (See Medallion Piecing Diagram.)

2. Cut border strips for the large triangles (D) from gold/green floral strip, 1½″ wide, and join to triangle sides. Join Seven Sisters blocks with triangles to form one large hexagon medallion. (See Medallion Piecing Diagram.)

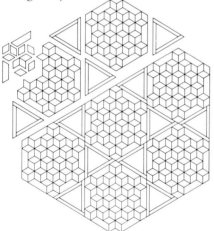

Medallion Piecing Diagram

3. Cut 4 *right* triangles with hypotenuse equal to the length of one side of hexagon medallion from cream fabric. Join to Seven Sisters medallion to form large rectangle.

4. For corner blocks, make a "square within a square" using 1 square (E) and 4 triangles (F). Make 4 blocks. Cut 4 border strips, 3½″ wide, from green/red floral stripe.

Join corner blocks to ends of 2 border strips, and join strips to quilt.

5. Piece 104 four-patch blocks of 1″ red and green squares (C) for second border. Join pieces at sides to form a diagonal strip as follows: 1 cream triangle (G), 1 cream print square (H), 1 four-patch block, 1 cream print square (H), and 1 cream triangle (G). Sew strips together along diagonal edge to form a border strip, and join to quilt. Diagonal strips will meet at corners in a mitered fashion.

6. For last border, make a "square within a square" using 1 square (I) and 4 triangles (J). Make 8 blocks, for midpoints and corners. Cut 8 border strips, 4″ wide, from green/ black floral stripe. Join 2 border strips, of equal length, with a "square within a square" block. Make 4 border strips with block positioned at midpoint of quilt sides. Join corner blocks to ends of 2 border strips, and join to quilt.

Quilting

Quilt ¼″ inside seam line of all diamonds. Duplicate diamond shape by quilting ¼″ from first quilting line inside diamonds. Quilt large triangles with Charlotte's original stylized trefoil design. Quilt ¼″ inside all remaining seam lines of medallion. Quilt parallel quilting lines ¾″ apart, to radiate from hexagon edge to outline quilting along first border. Quilt a 1″ cross-hatching pattern on second border. Floral print borders are quilted along stripes and floral design to enhance the fabric's pattern.

Finished Edges

Bind with red fabric.

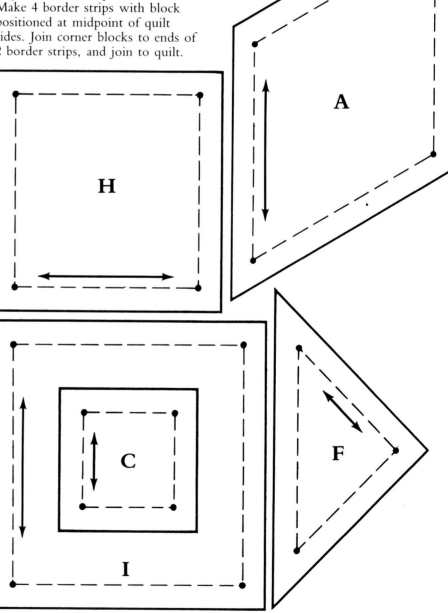

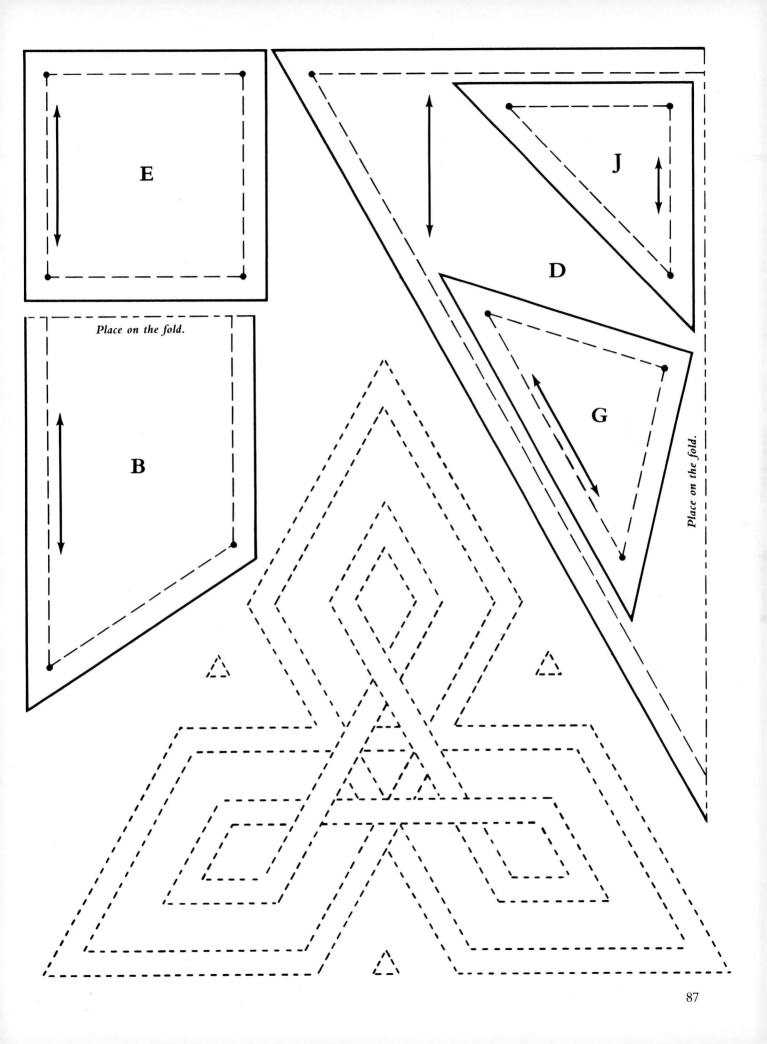

E

Place on the fold.

B

J

D

G

Place on the fold.

Rose B. Glass

Port Hueneme, California

Rose carries pictures of her quilts in her purse, just like grand-children, and drags them out every chance she gets! "I do love quilting," writes Rose. "I've been an off-and-on quilter for the last 30 years. I always say I am retiring, but I know I'll be making another quilt." We know friends and family are glad to hear that, since she gives most of her quilts to them.

Like most Californians, Rose is transplanted from elsewhere. She grew up in North Dakota, married and moved to Wisconsin in 1925, and settled in California in the sixties. California is now home. "I'm real happy, and no snow to shovel," says Rose. She loves to travel, having made trips to China, Ireland, Scotland, and England in the last few years, gathering inspiration for quilt designs along the way. She plays bridge once or twice a week, and is trying her hand at calligraphy. At this pace, Rose is still a youngster at 84 with a lot of quilting ahead of her.

Corinth
1980

Rose's inspiration for *Corinth* came from a postcard she bought in Corinth, Greece (hence the name), depicting a mosaic floor in a Roman villa, laid in 250 B.C. With a yard-stick, in which she bored holes for accurate measurements, Rose drafted the circular mosaic design that graces the center of her quilt. From that, cardboard templates and a "road map" for color placement were made. Cut on the bias, mosaic triangles should give easily, if necessary, to fit into circular layers. Rose's story sends a message to all quilters: that is, inspiration for quilt designs lies in all sorts of places, just waiting to be lifted to a quilted format. All it takes is a little ingenuity, and a willing and positive attitude, to tackle any project that you've imagined.

Corinth

Finished Quilt Size
80" x 100"

Fabric Requirements

Blue	—5 yd.
Light blue	—3¾ yd.
Tan	—5¼ yd.
Blue print	—2 yd.
Cream	—3¼ yd.
Binding	—1¼ yd.
Backing	—6 yd.

Number to Cut

Template A1	—12 blue
	12 blue print
	8 tan
Template A2	—32 cream
Template B1	—16 blue
	8 blue print
	8 tan
Template B2	—32 cream
Template C1	—16 blue
	8 blue print
	8 tan
Template C2	—32 cream
Template D1	—16 blue
	8 blue print
	8 tan
Template D2	—32 cream
Template E1	—12 blue
	8 blue print
	12 tan
Template E2	—32 cream
Template F1	—16 blue
	8 blue print
	8 tan
Template F2	—32 cream
Template G1	—12 blue
	12 blue print
	8 tan
Template G2	—32 cream

Template H1 — 8 blue
12 blue print
12 tan
Template H2 — 32 cream
Template I1 — 8 blue
12 blue print
12 tan
Template I2 — 32 cream
Template J1 — 8 blue
16 blue print
8 tan
Template J2 — 32 cream
Template K1 — 12 blue
8 blue print
12 tan
Template K2 — 32 cream
Template L1 — 16 blue
8 blue print
8 tan
Template L2 — 32 cream
Template M1 — 12 blue
12 blue print
8 tan
Template M2 — 32 cream
Template N — 32 blue
Template O — 36 blue
12 blue print
12 tan
60 cream
Template P — 310 light blue
310 tan
Template Q — 310 blue print
Template R — 8 light blue

Quilt Top Assembly

1. Piece triangles A1 to A2 at sides to form first mosaic circle. Refer to photograph for proper color placement. Continue to piece triangles to form concentric circles. B1 and B2 form the second circle, C1 and C2 form the third circle, and so forth, ending with M1 and M2. As each circle is completed, join it to the previous circle. Note: Each triangle is cut so that the bias edge forms the arc of the circle, and pieces should give easily to fit around the circle if necessary.
2. Cut tan bias strip 2¼″ wide to encircle mosaic medallion, and join.
3. Join triangles (N) to medallion edge.
4. Cut a circle from blue, 8½″ in diameter, and appliqué to center of mosaic medallion.
5. Cut 2 background pieces from light blue, 36¾″ x 53″, and join lengthwise. Fold into quarters, and finger-crease to find center. Center mosaic medallion on top, pin, and appliqué to background. Trim background fabric underneath

medallion to ¼″ seam allowance.
6. Piece 30 triangles (O) for each corner section. Refer to photograph for color placement. Make 4 sections. Lay each section on background fabric at corners, and appliqué to background. Trim background fabric underneath triangles to ¼″ seam allowance.
7. Cut 4 border strips from cream fabric, 1″ wide, join to quilt, and miter corners.
8. Cut 4 border strips from tan fabric, 1¾″ wide, join to quilt, and miter corners.
9. Cut 4 border strips from blue fabric, 6½″ wide, join to quilt, and miter corners.
10. Join 2 template Ps to each diagonal edge of template Q to form one section of the pieced border. Join sections at sides to form border

strips. Make border strips for sides and top and bottom of quilt. Join 2 triangles (R) to form corner square. Make 4. Join 2 corner squares to the ends of 2 pieced border strips. Join border strips to quilt.
11. Cut 4 border strips, 4¼″ wide, from blue fabric, join to quilt, and miter corners.

Quilting

Outline-quilt ¼″ inside seam line of all triangles and shapes of pieced border. Refer to Quilting Diagram for medallion background quilting. Outline-quilt ¼″ inside seam lines of first and second borders. Quilt 1½″ square cross-hatching on last border strip.

Finished Edges

Bind with blue fabric.

Quilting Diagram

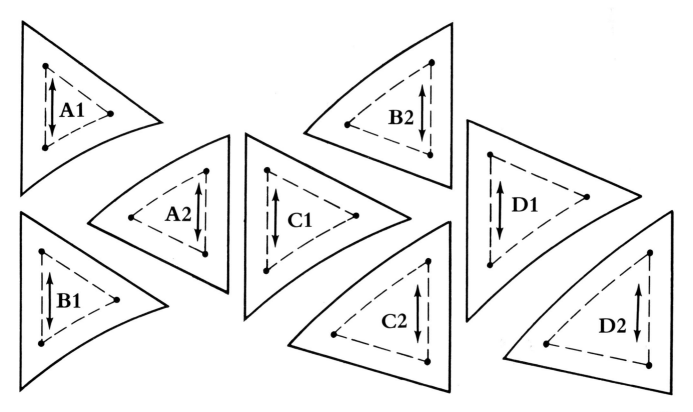

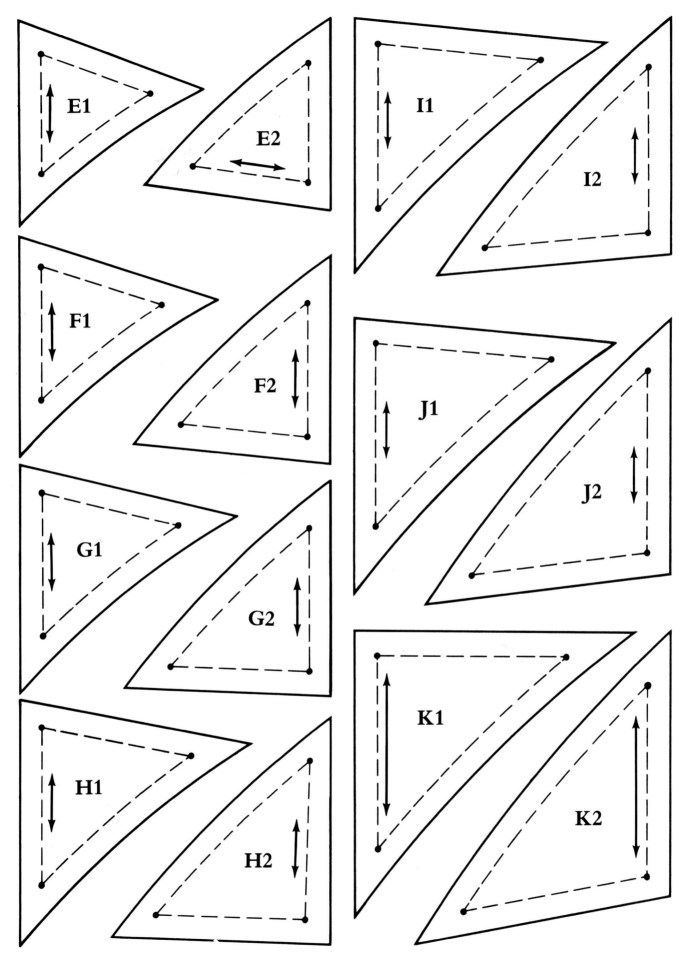

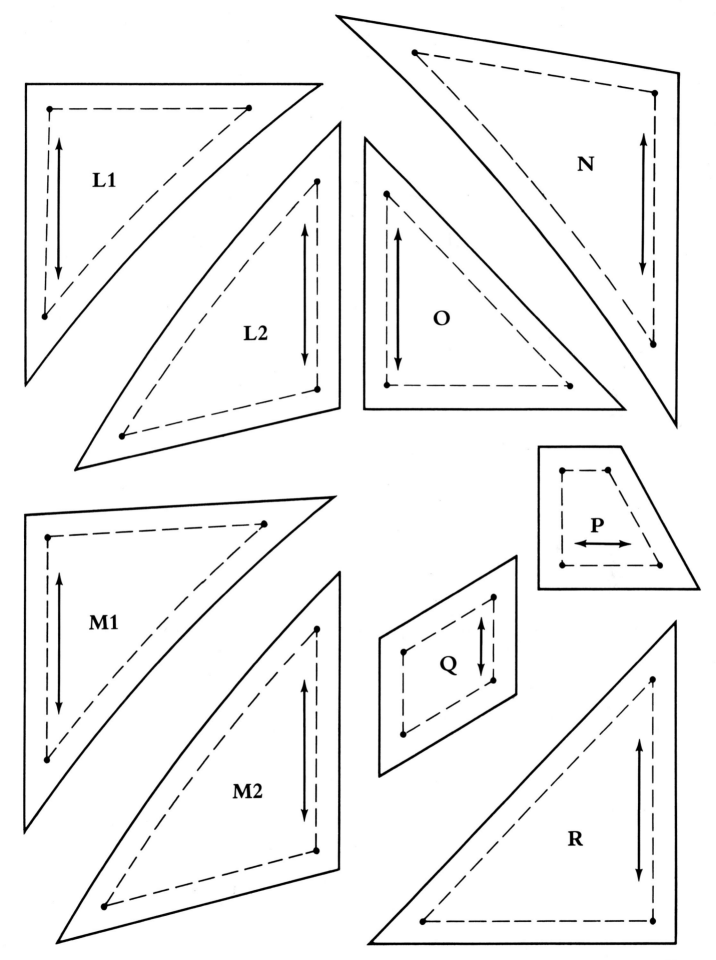

Jo Diggs
Portland, Maine

A dedication to embroidery and a move to Albuquerque were the catalysts that helped make Jo Diggs the superb appliqué artist she is today. Once she viewed the brightly colored reversed appliqué of the Cuna Indians of Panama, her former interest in embroidery took a back seat to what has become an enduring romance with appliqué. "Appliqué gives me the freedom that piecing doesn't offer, to achieve representative images." Jo confesses, "I sew most of the time, can't live without it, and do anything else I do (except eating chocolate) with the view of 'how soon can I get back to my sewing' (which is always appliqué)."

As an artist, Jo is sensitive to the need for freedom of expression in all design, including quilts. Therefore, instead of giving exact fabric requirements and patterns for these two quilts, she is sharing instructions for the layering technique of appliqué (see page 96). Jo wants quilters to use the layering technique of appliqué as a method of building a design, by letting the fabric and imagination create a quilt just as an artist would paint on a canvas.

Portion of
**Mother Earth,
Father Sky II**

Mother Earth, Father Sky II
1985

Mother Earth, Father Sky II is a composite of many landscapes Jo has seen and even sewn on garments she has made. "It was such a triumph to actually finish it and have it look so good," says Jo. "There was one point when I almost threw it away, because I thought I would never finish it! But six years after starting, I did finish, and everything except one of the small panels was left as I originally cut it out."

Jo hopes this portion of *Mother Earth, Father Sky II* that she is sharing with you will entice you to expand upon it, and create a Mother Earth of your own. "Landscapes and the multi-layered technique just seem to work well together," explains Jo.

A portion of *Mother Earth* is shown at left with the levels of layering indicated, to aid you with your appliqué. All quilting is done in-the-ditch, except where indicated otherwise.

Basic Instructions for Layering Technique of Appliqué

Cut muslin to the size of quilt desired. Begin by cutting pieces for large areas first, and lay out the complete landscape before stitching. Pin sections together, and remove all layers except the bottom one, so that you will begin stitching on the layer that touches the background (Figure 1). Appliqué, and press shape flat when stitching is completed. Pin the next layer into place, and appliqué. After the second layer is stitched, lift it up and trim away the underlap of the first layer, so that its edge is a fraction wider than the turned-under edge of the appliqué (Figure 2). Jo recommends doing this to prevent the ridges of any fabric underneath from showing, especially after appliqué is pressed. Press second layer. Repeat for each subsequent layer (Figure 3). Increase the number of stitches in curved and corner areas for reinforcement. Clip curve and corner seam allowances to ease appliquéd edge.

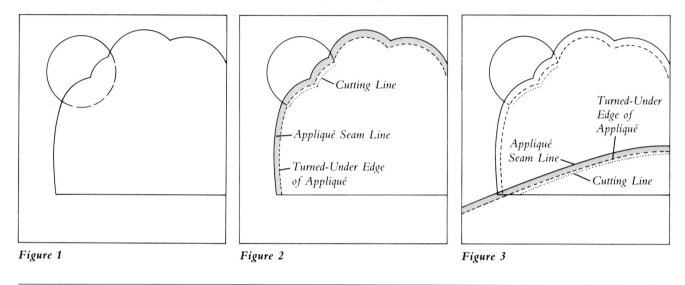

Figure 1   Figure 2   Figure 3

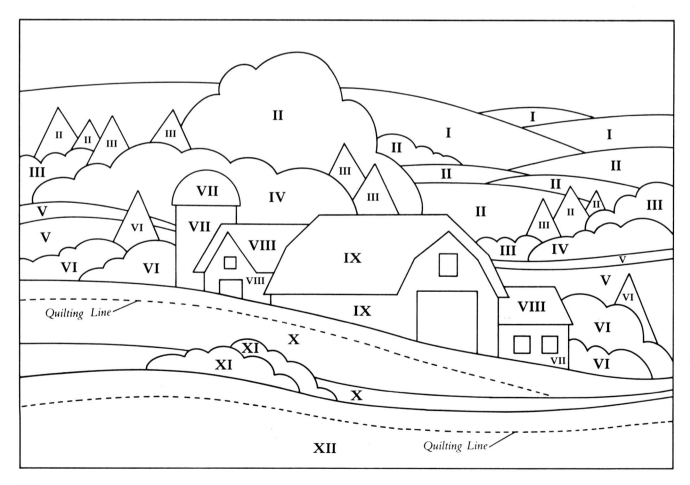

Snowscape
1984

"I wanted to make this quilt to show how I had adjusted to living in New England after living in New Mexico," says Jo. "It was a very difficult transition for me, and this quilt marked my full recovery." *Snowscape* is appropriately made entirely of wool. The textures and weaves of wool perfectly emulate the undulations of snowy terrains and hearth-warmed mountain cabins. Jo also tells us wool is a "very forgiving" material to work with. By steam pressing, a multitude of puffy places will flatten out instantly.

Snowscape was awarded Best of Show and Exceptional Merit at the 1984 Vermont Quilt Festival. Jo shares a portion of it here. Layering level numbers are indicated on the diagram (see drawing at left), to aid you with your appliqué. All quilting is done in-the-ditch, except where indicated otherwise.

***Portion of* Snowscape**

With two small boys, ages four and five, Betsy needed something just for herself. Having a need for a new creative outlet, Betsy organized her own quilting class, found a teacher and a babysitter, so that the children would be busy, and proceeded to learn to quilt. That was some 10 years ago, and of the 10 original students, six are still very active quilters.

A year after organizing the class, and a few ribbons later, Betsy decided she wanted to become more involved in quilting, and challenged herself to make a very difficult quilt. That quilt, the *Basket Quilt,* won the Judges' Choice Trophy for the Eastern States Exposition Craft Adventure in Springfield, Massachusetts. With duly earned confidence, Betsy began teaching others to quilt, and now considers it one of the main joys of quilting. Betsy claims, "Besides my own personal creative satisfaction, there is the joy of seeing others find this within themselves."

Betsy Henebry
East Hartland, Connecticut

As I Wait
1985
Betsy can tell you all about the old expression: "Hurry up and wait." One day she decided to take the useless "sport" of waiting and turn it into quiltmaking time. Over a period of six years, hours spent waiting for her boys at Little League games, skiing, or swimming became hand-piecing opportunities. Borders were added in car garages, or doctors' offices, and during a special family trip to Vermont. The life span of piecing *As I Wait* equals her two boys' elementary school years! "It is a very special and precious quilt for me because of the years and memories that it represents," says Betsy. It was a first prize winner at the Eastern States Exposition Craft Adventure in Springfield, Massachusetts, in 1985.

Betsy used Mountain Mist's Pomegranate pattern (see our Resource Section) for the center medallion, and refreshingly integrated pieced-block borders to complement her pomegranate vine.

As I Wait

Finished Quilt Size
99¾" x 99¾"

Number of Blocks and Finished Size
1 center block—6" x 6"
24 Windmill blocks—6" x 6" each
32 Hourglass blocks—7" x 7" each

Fabric Requirements

Navy print — 4¾ yd.
Red print — 5 yd.
Cream print — 3 yd.
Muslin — 3 yd.
Red print
for binding — 1¼ yd.
Muslin for backing — 9 yd.

Number to Cut

Template A — 104 red print
104 cream print
Template B — 512 cream print
256 blue print
Template C — 96 blue print
Template D — 8 red print
Template E — 60 red print
Template F — 128 blue print
Template G — 12 red print
Template G★ — 12 red print
Template H — 32 red print
Template I — 20 red print
Template J — 12 cream print
Template K — 32 cream print
Template L — 80 cream print
Template M — 12 blue print
Template M★ — 12 blue print
Template N — 32 blue print
Template N★ — 32 blue print
Template O — 32 blue print

★ — Flip or turn over template if
fabric is one-sided.

Quilt Top Assembly

1. From muslin, cut four 14½"
squares. Locate center of block, and
position pomegranate pattern on the
diagonal, as shown, so that stem
extends from one corner of the
block. Mark pomegranate position,
and appliqué to muslin. Repeat for
each block.
2. Join muslin squares to form one
large square.
3. Join triangles (A) of red and
cream fabric for center block. (See
Center Block Piecing Diagram.) Set
block diagonally, center over point
where the 4 muslin squares meet,
and appliqué.

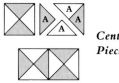

*Center Block
Piecing Diagram*

4. Cut 4 border strips from red fabric, 1½" x 30½". Join a strip to
each side of large appliquéd muslin
square, and miter corners.
5. First Pieced Border: Join triangles
(A and C) of red, cream, and navy
fabric, to complete Windmill block.

(See Windmill Block Piecing Diagram.) Make 24 Windmill blocks.

*Windmill
Block Piecing
Diagram*

Make 2 border rows with 5 Windmill blocks each, and 2 rows with 7
Windmill blocks. Join borders with
5 Windmill blocks to opposite sides
of quilt, and borders with 7 Windmill blocks to top and bottom.
6. Cut 4 border strips from red fabric, 1½" x 42½". Cut four 1½"
squares from navy fabric. Join
squares to the ends of 2 strips. Join
the strips without navy squares to
the sides of the quilt top. Join the
strips with navy squares to the top
and bottom.
7. Appliquéd Border: Cut 4 strips
from muslin, 10½" x 64½". Join to
quilt top, and miter corners. Appliqué pomegranate vine to muslin
border.
8. Cut 4 border strips from navy
fabric, 2" x 67½", join to quilt, and
miter corners.
9. Cut 4 border strips from cream
fabric, 1½" x 69½", join to quilt,
and miter corners.
10. Second Pieced Border: Join
triangles (B) and squares (F) of
navy and cream fabric to complete
Hourglass block. (See Hourglass
Block Piecing Diagram.) Make 32
blocks. For border rows, alternate
diagonally set Hourglass blocks
with triangle E. Nine blocks should

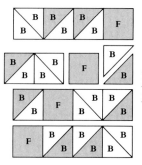

*Hourglass
Block Piecing
Diagram*

fit on sides, and 7 blocks each for
top and bottom. Set corners of borders with triangle D.
11. Cut 4 border strips from cream
fabric, 2" wide, join to quilt, and
miter corners.
12. Cut 4 border strips from navy
fabric, 4½" wide, join to quilt, and
miter corners.

Quilting

Outline-quilt ¼″ inside seam line of triangles of center block, Windmill blocks, and Hourglass blocks. Outline-quilt ¼″ inside seam line of cream center of each pomegranate. Outline-quilt ¼″ inside seam line of cream centers of each red flower on border. Quilt pomegranate pattern within each red print triangle of second pieced border, quilting a half-pattern for corners. Remaining areas are quilted with a 1″-square cross-hatching pattern.

Finished Edges

Bind with red print fabric.

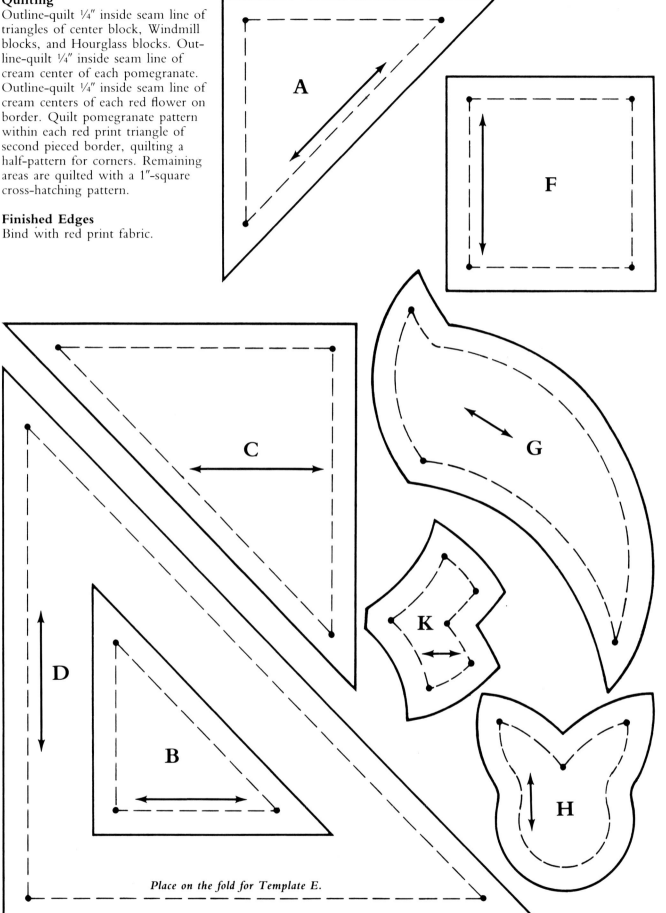

Place on the fold for Template E.

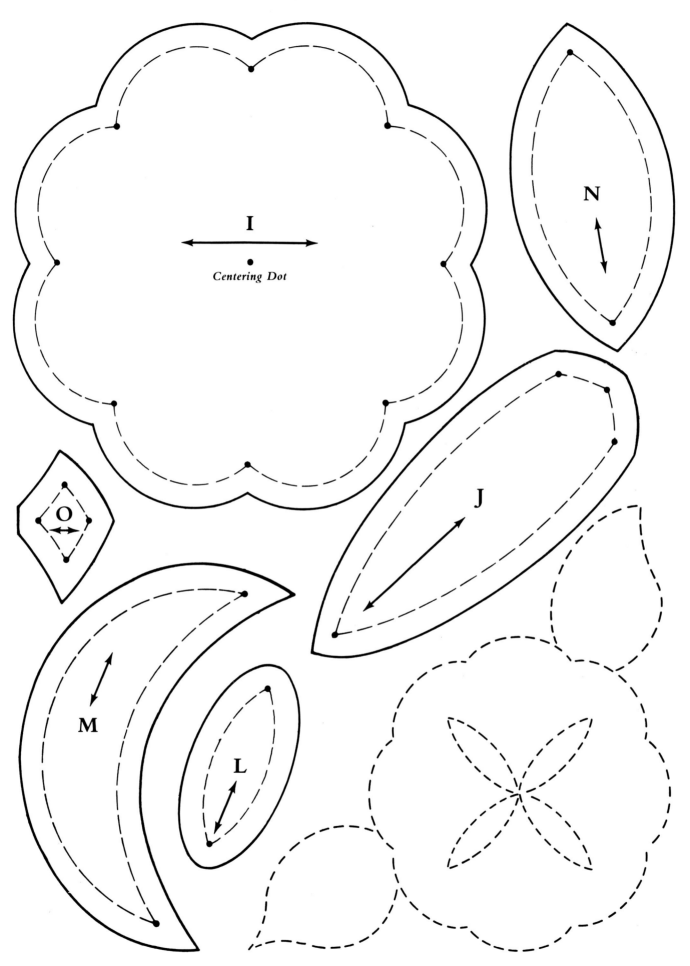

I

Centering Dot

N

J

O

M

L

TRADITIONS IN QUILTING

From generation to generation young girls were taught to sew as soon as they were able to hold a needle. Until recent times, that first stitched article was often a simple patchwork quilt. As a young girl improved her technique and gained confidence, she was taught the more complicated steps of designing and quilting, to prepare her for the day when she would be the teacher.

Though such hands-on sewing lessons are rare today or are left to formal classrooms, the fondest memories of many of our present-day quilters are those of their mothers or grandmothers quilting. Today's quilters remember well the twinkle in mother's eye and the pride on grandmother's face when hours of stitching culminated in beauty and warmth. The quilting tradition is enshrined in those memories of joyful expressions on satisfied faces. Each quilter has her story to tell—many similar to others, but with a slight variation, a twist that makes the quilting story in her life just a little different. And somehow, we never grow tired of hearing them.

Sisters (left to right)—
Betty Roberts,
Geneva Smith,
Peggy Sharp,
Annette Byrd,
and Geraldine Tyler—
admire Geneva's quilting
on the 1870s
Seven Sisters quilt.

Seven Sisters
Top pieced 1870s,
Quilted 1986

One sunny southern day, Geneva's friend Sarah Gilbreath handed her a quilt top that Sarah had found in her mother's belongings. Sarah, a retired schoolteacher, doesn't quilt, and neither did her mother, but she knew Geneva could help her. Geneva was delighted and couldn't wait to quilt it.

Because of the fabric, and especially the colors and pattern selection, it is believed the top was pieced around the time of this country's centennial. Sarah believes her grandmother pieced most of the quilt, but suspects some of the piecing was done by others, because stitching and piece sizes vary from block to block.

Stored in a trunk over the years, the quilt top was in near-perfect condition. Geneva lovingly added new borders to secure ragged edges and to enlarge it just a bit. When the layering was complete, she meticulously carried her quilting thread through the seasoned portals of woven fabric. She admits it was a little hard to quilt because of the quality of fabric, but loved every minute of it. "I enjoyed quilting this old quilt because I knew someone had started a beautiful quilt and was never able to finish it. I knew they must have loved quilts as I do. My only sorrow is that the person who pieced the top can never see the finished quilt."

Geneva Smith
Fort Payne, Alabama

Atop the rolling landscape of northern Alabama sits Acorn Hills Farm, Geneva Smith's home and often the setting for family quilt shows. Geneva has been quilting for over 14 years, and especially enjoys sitting by the fire and piecing on a wintry day. But no story about Geneva would be complete without including her four sisters and the quilting tradition that intertwines their sisterhood.

The sisters gained a love and respect for quilting from their mother, Lydia Woods, who raised nine children, and quilted out of necessity, piecing feed and flour sacks, carding the cotton for batting, and using the twine from the feed sacks for quilting thread. "At the time, I did not realize it was a necessity," remembers Peggy, the youngest sister. "Mother would quilt late at night and seemed to never tire of it. I believe she enjoyed it so much, it was never a chore to her." (Quilting was also a tradition in Lydia's life, for her mother and sisters all made quilts.)

Geraldine, the oldest sister, is the only one of the daughters who learned to piece and quilt from her mother. "When I was a little girl, my mother would cut squares for me to piece, and I always loved to do it," says Geraldine.

Since they live near each other, the sisters' quilting is part of the cement that binds their relationship. Peggy, the last to start quilting, admits, "I felt left out, and quilting is one of the qualifications of being one of them. I decided if I was going to be included in their conversations and activities, I had better get started."

Their biggest enjoyment is sharing their quilting, not only with each other, but also with their friends. These industrious sisters have held three family quilt shows to display their quilts. "We call and invite friends who like quilting," says Betty, who has hosted two shows at her home.

Among the five of them, the sisters have completed over 70 quilts, but none of the sisters considers herself a professional. Annette, who teaches quilting and is president of the Quilt Lovers Guild in Hartselle, Alabama, sells some of her quilts, but confesses, "It is very hard to part with one. It's like losing one of your best friends." Betty speaks for all of them when she says, "I am not a professional. I just like to make quilts."

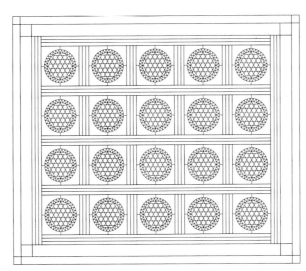

Seven Sisters

Finished Quilt Size
97½″ x 117″

Number of Blocks and Finished Size
20 blocks—16¼″ x 16¼″ each

Fabric Requirements
Navy   —7¼ yd.
Burgundy   —6¾ yd.
Muslin   —5½ yd.
Burgundy for
    binding   —1¼ yd.
Muslin for backing —9¾ yd.

Number to Cut
Template A   —140 burgundy
                      240 muslin
Template B   —840 navy
Template C   —240 muslin
Template D   —640 burgundy
Template E   —640 navy
Template F   —80 muslin

Quilt Top Assembly
1. Though machine piecing may be done, for accuracy Geneva recommends hand piecing the block, using the paper-piecing method for the hexagons. Begin with the center star, joining 6 triangles (B) to hexagons (A). Join all but one triangle to each of the outside hexagons, to form a large pieced hexagon. (See Block Diagram.)

Join 2 of template C to the sides of triangle (B) to make an arc. Make 6. Join to sides of each hexagon to form circle.

To form a pieced ring, alternate triangles (D and E), and join at sides so that curved edge of triangle E is on the outside. Join pieced circle to Seven Sisters circle. Join 4 of

template F together at short sides. Join to circle to complete block. Make 20 blocks.
2. Cut sashing strips 1⅝″ x 16¾″: 10 from navy and 16 from burgundy. Join lengthwise 2 navy strips with a burgundy strip in the center. Make 16 sashing pieces.
3. Alternate 5 blocks with 4 sashing pieces, beginning with a block to form a row. Make 4 rows.
4. Cut sashing strips for length of each row 1⅝″ wide: 10 navy and 5 burgundy. Join as before, making 5

sashing strips. Join sashing pieces to both sides of each row.
5. Cut sashing strips for top and bottom of quilt, 1⅝″ wide: 4 navy and 2 burgundy. Join as before, making 2 sashing strips. Join to top and bottom of quilt.
6. From muslin, cut 4 border strips, 5″ wide. Cut four 5″ squares. Join squares to ends of shorter border strips. Join borders to quilt.
7. From burgundy fabric, cut 4 borders, 3¾″ wide. Cut four 3½″ squares. Join squares to ends of shorter border strips. Join borders to quilt.

Quilting
Outline-quilt ⅛″ inside seam line of hexagons and triangles. Outline-quilt ¼″ inside seam lines of all sashing and border strips. Geneva chose a leaf quilting pattern for the muslin strips and a flower design for the muslin squares. Bars of quilting are formed by quilting parallel lines 1¼″ apart along burgundy border.

Finished Edges
Bind with burgundy fabric.

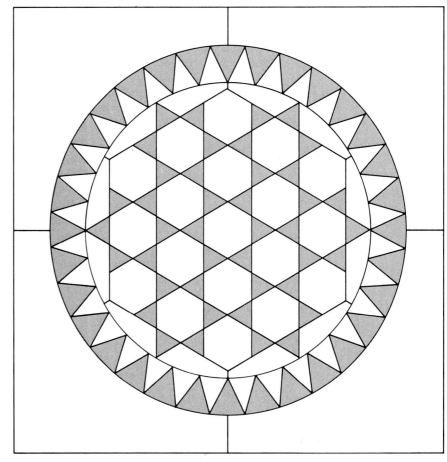

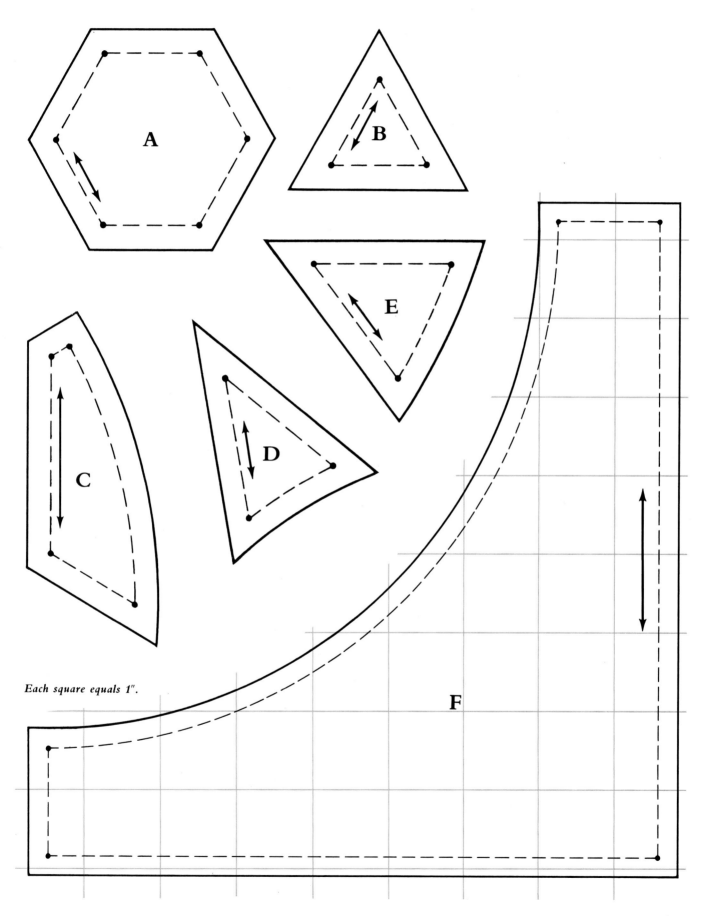

A

B

E

C

D

Each square equals 1".

F

Rosalie H. Bourland

Converse, Texas

Over the past 10 years, Rosalie has learned "most everything I know about quilting" from her mother-in-law, Ethel Bourland. Ethel's mother and grandmother were quilters, too, and at 87, Ethel still pieces quilts. But the quilting itself is sometimes difficult for her, and many of her tops are quilted by Rosalie. In doing this quilting, Rosalie provides the link that keeps the Bourland quilting tradition alive.

After working in an office for 28 years, Rosalie now makes time for her quilting by operating a small quilt shop and teaching quilting at her General Store in Converse. Although she has always sewn using the sewing machine, for quilting projects she prefers handwork. This allows her to quilt while she travels, carrying what she calls her fly-away kit. Organized with needles, pins, scissors, thread, and plenty of things to quilt, she quilts in car garages, quilt shows, and once on a trip around the globe. "We were gone for 30 days—I made every minute count," brags Rosalie. She enjoys the new friends she makes while quilting in airport lobbies. "Even though there may be no verbal communication because of the language barriers, there seems to be a mutual understanding and friendship, with many nods of approval," says Rosalie.

Twinkling Stars Over Texas

Top pieced 1912,
Quilted 1986

As I looked up at those beautiful, twinkling stars, and then finally the awesome comet, several things suddenly occurred to me. Is that why you chose the star pattern—because you liked the peaceful night time that gave respite from the south Texas heat? I'm told that the climate around Hearne, where you lived, was so hot and sultry that your family had to pick the cotton by moonlight—after the sun went down and the ground cooled. So you must have known the stars well and loved them. You knew, too, that stars seem to twinkle different colors, because you included many shades of red throughout your beautiful quilt top.

Twinkling Stars over Texas was one of the quilt tops given to Rosalie for quilting by her mother-in-law, Ethel Bourland. The top was pieced by Ethel's mother, Lucy Harris, sometime between 1912 and 1916. The pattern is believed to be a Twinkling Star variation, with plenty of pivot points that will test your skill in turning corners.

As Rosalie quilted Lucy's masterpiece, she felt so close to Lucy that it was almost as though Lucy were watching over Rosalie's shoulder, urging her on. Not much is known about Lucy, except that she was a farmer's wife, and her mother also quilted and demanded perfection in all aspects of sewing.

When Rosalie completed the quilt, an obligation overwhelmed her to write an imaginary letter to Lucy and share her thoughts and frustrations with her. The above is excerpted from Rosalie's letter.

Her letter continues: "I want to tell you that I think you did a perfectly super job piecing your quilt top. How you managed to do so well, using the heavy feed sack string, is beyond me. I just wonder how long you worked on the top—the pieces were so small.

"Well, after 74 years, your quilt is finally finished. I sure did enjoy working on it, even if there were 252 of those stars. You know, while most quilts have one lifetime of innermost thoughts and secrets sewn within their stitches, this one has two: yours and mine. We treasure this quilt, promise to take care of it, and pass it along from generation to generation until it is so tattered and threadbare that the stars no longer twinkle."

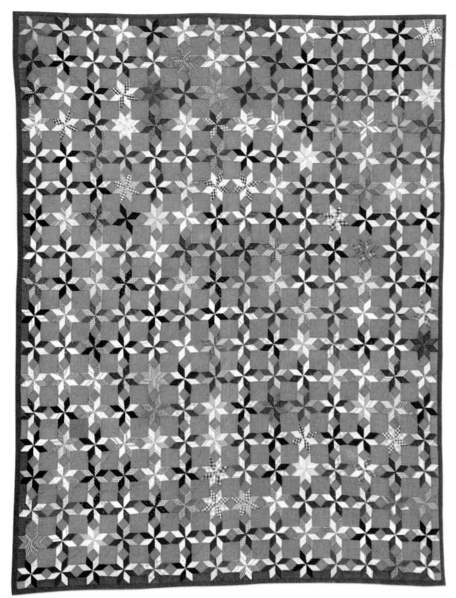

Quilt Top Assembly

1. Complete the eight-pointed star by joining sides of 8 diamonds (A). (See Star Piecing Diagram.) Alternate light and dark scrap diamonds to make your stars twinkle. Make 252 stars!

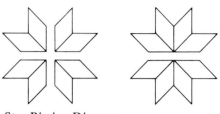

Star Piecing Diagram

2. Alternate 14 stars with 13 squares (B), and join to form a row. Begin and end each row with a triangle (E). (See Star Row Piecing Diagram.) Make 18 star rows.

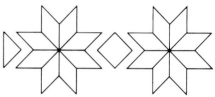

Star Row Piecing Diagram

3. Join star rows by alternating squares B and C. (See Final Assembly Diagram.) Square B will fill the space where star points meet. Begin and end rows with rectangle D. Use templates B, D, and E for the first and last rows.

Twinkling Stars over Texas

Finished Quilt Size
75″ x 96″

Fabric Requirements
Blue   —4¼ yd.
Light and dark
  scraps   —8¾ yd.
Blue for binding   —1¼ yd.
Muslin for backing —5½ yd.

Number to Cut
Template A   —2,016 scrap
                            fabrics
Template B   —476 blue
Template C   —221 blue
Template D   —60 blue
Template E   —64 blue

Final Assembly Diagram

Quilting
Outline-quilt ¼″ inside all seam lines.

Finished Edges
Bind with blue fabric.

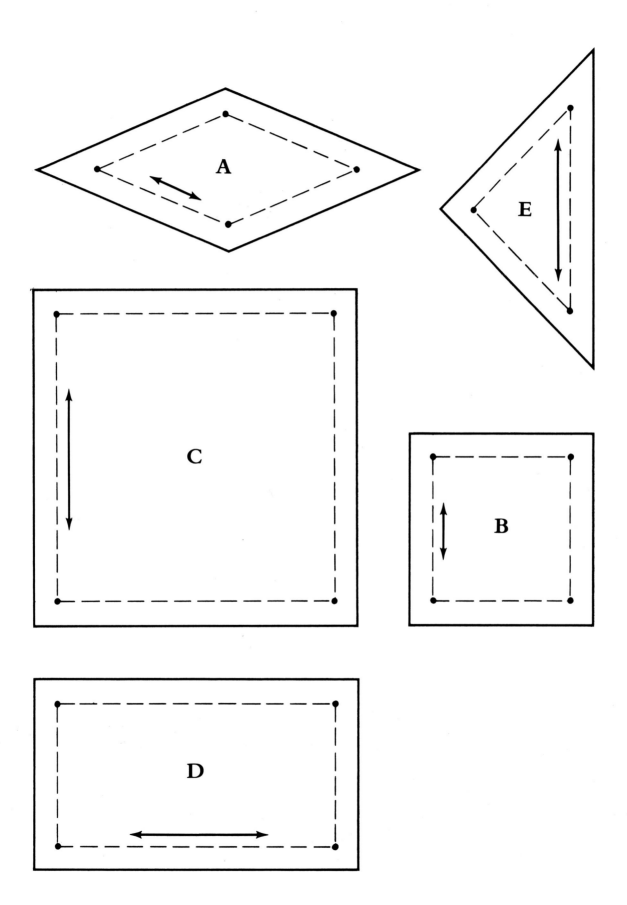

Iantha (Tiny) Powers

Mt. Olive, Alabama

Sit down with a glass of iced tea in Tiny's kitchen, and you will want to spend the day listening to Tiny tell you about her life and, of course, her quilting. (If you had been quilting for over 60 years, like Tiny, you'd have a lot to say about quilting, too.) Tiny is the ninth of 12 children, a farmer's daughter. Tiny's mother quilted, but with 12 children, she didn't have much time to spend teaching her girls to quilt. When Tiny was barely a teenager, her mother handed her a bundle of scraps to piece. With a little encouragement and a bit of advice to make her stitches small enough so "you can't catch a toenail," Tiny embarked on what has become a lifetime of glorious quilting.

Today, Tiny still lives in the house she and her husband moved into when they were married 50 years ago. She has two sons, five grandchildren, and one great-grandson. With only sons, none of whom quilt, Tiny spends much of her time sharing her quilting knowledge with women in her small town of Mt. Olive. One of Tiny's friends told us she wouldn't think of making a quilt without Tiny's advice and critique. "I bring all my quilting to Tiny for final inspection," she told us. If it doesn't pass Tiny's critique, she rips it out, and does it again until Tiny says it's okay.

Tiny was given her nickname by a second grade classmate because she had a tiny voice, but along with that tiny voice came a heart made of gold that loves to share her quilting.

Chicken Scratch Star
1982

"When I first saw the Chicken Scratch Star pattern, I thought someone was appliquéing lace on checks," says Tiny. Once she realized it was embroidery, she thought, "How really beautiful," and knew she had to make one. Tiny decided to combine it with her quilting expertise, and here it is as the *Chicken Scratch Star* quilt. The Chicken Scratch Star embroidery pattern seems to have been around for some time, but we so liked the marvelous way in which Tiny combined her embroidery, quilting patterns, and colors that we felt you would enjoy it, too. The pattern will change its appearance according to the size of the gingham checks. "There are no short-cuts to embroidering these stars," says Tiny. "They take time and patience, but the result is worth it."

Chicken Scratch Star

Finished Quilt Size
76" x 94"

Number of Blocks and Finished Size
20 blocks—14" x 14" each

Fabric Requirements
Black-and-white
  gingham   —4½ yd.
Black   —3¼ yd.
Red for backing
  and binding   —5½ yd.

Embroidery Floss
75 skeins white
10 skeins red

Quilt Top Assembly
1. Cut twenty 14½" gingham squares. Fold each square into quarters, and finger-crease to find the center.
2. Embroider each large gingham square with a Chicken Scratch Star in the center as follows:

(1) To establish the center of your Chicken Scratch Star, use 2 or 3 strands of red thread and make a star stitch in the white gingham square found in the very center of your 14½" square. Surround this stitch with a red star stitch in each of 8 white gingham squares to form a box. (See the Star Stitch Outline Diagram.)

(2) With 2 or 3 strands of white thread, make a star stitch in each black square of gingham, as shown in Star Stitch Diamond Diagram, to form a diamond. Continue around the red square, and complete 8 diamonds to form a star.

(3) Outline each diamond with a red star stitch in each white square. (See Star Stitch Outline and Star Stitch Diamond Diagram.)

(4) Circle Stitches: With 3 strands of white thread, make straight running stitches going over each gray square and under each white square within each diamond (Running Stitch Diagram). Using 6 strands of white thread, bring the needle up on one side of a gray square, and make a circle around each white square by going under each running stitch. Return the needle down the entrance hole to complete the circle. Continue until each diamond is filled with circle stitches. (See Circle Stitch Diagrams.)

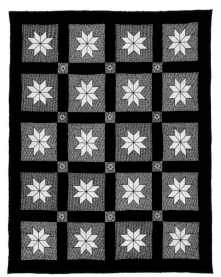

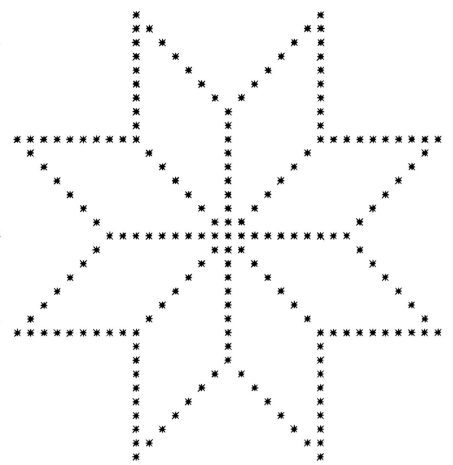

Star Stitch Outline Diagram

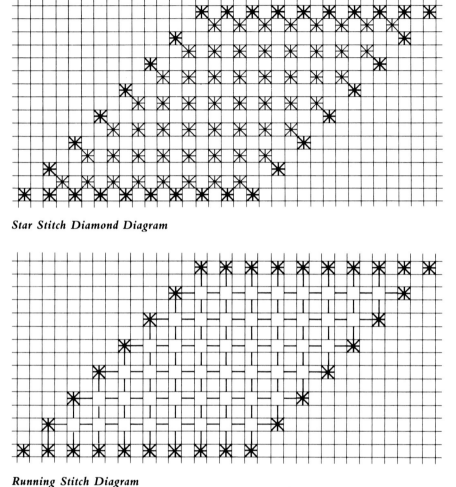

Star Stitch Diamond Diagram

3. Cut twelve 4½" gingham squares. Embroider a small Chicken Scratch Star in each as above.
4. Cut 31 black sashing strips, 4½" x 14½".
5. Alternate 4 large gingham squares with 3 black sashing strips and join, beginning with a sashing strip to form a row. Make 5 rows.
6. Alternate 3 small gingham squares with 4 black sashing strips and join, beginning with a sashing strip to form a row. Make 4 rows.
7. Alternate large gingham square rows with sashing rows and join, beginning with a sashing row.
8. Cut 4 black border strips, 4½" wide, join to quilt, and miter the corners.
9. Cut quilt backing large enough to roll hem.

Quilting

Outline-quilt outside embroidered edges of all Chicken Scratch Stars. Choose your favorite quilting pattern for the black sashing and borders, or select a floral vine pattern, as Tiny did.

Finished Edges

Tiny rolled 1½" of red backing to the front, turned edge under ¼", and secured with a slipstitch to bind quilt.

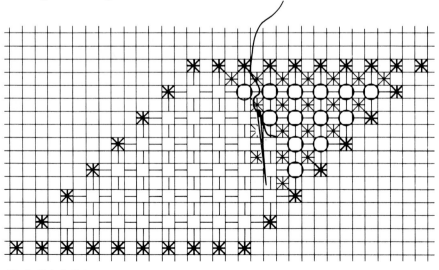

Running Stitch Diagram

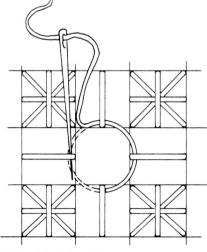

Circle Stitch Detail

Circle Stitch Diagram

115

Sandy McLeon

Grapevine, Texas

Sandy's memories of quilting go back to the days when her father planted and picked the cotton, and her mother carded it to remove the burrs and grass to make the batting. "Men came to visit, and the ladies would go in a separate room and quilt," says Sandy. Fabric at seven cents a yard was expensive then. That may be the reason Sandy collected scraps of fabric long before she quilted. A 39th birthday and an enjoyment of crafts and anything artistic were reasons enough for Sandy to undertake a new hobby, quilting. With plenty of fabrics on hand and a working knowledge of quilting, she decided to try it. "It was always on my mind," remembers Sandy. "It's in your blood."

Now that her two children are grown, she and her husband are alone again and "loving it!" she exclaims. "Quilting gives me the pleasure and sense of peace and joy of creating; it preserves my sanity," says Sandy. She is working on her 12th quilt in six years, and has more planned. Sandy muses, "I hope to live long enough to use up my collection of fabrics."

Indian Squaw

Finished Quilt Size
68½" x 95"

Number of Blocks and Finished Size
20 blocks—14" x 16" each

Fabric Requirements
Black	— ¼ yd.
Peach	—3½ yd.
Black/peach print	—2 yd.
Cotton scraps	—2½ yd.
Black for binding	—1¼ yd.
Muslin for backing	—5½ yd.

Indian Squaw Trims
Assorted fringes	—5½ yd. total
Assorted braids, rickrack, ribbons	—5 yd. total
Black yarn	—4 oz. skein
Contrasting yarns/ribbons for hair braids	

Indian Squaw
1983

Twenty colorfully bedecked Indian squaws rest calmly in their individual brilliant-peach blocks, surrounded by contrasting black sashing. We suspect, though, that these Indian squaws did some traveling before they settled on this quilt, since Sandy told us she loves to appliqué and does so anywhere she is at the moment.

Sandy prefers to take traditional patterns, such as *Indian Squaw*, and elaborate upon them. Each squaw is a freehand drawing and placed to face Sandy's shining sun. Other original touches include symbolic quilting patterns: a cactus that represents trouble; an armadillo that represents humor; a snake, suggesting caution where one walks; a

roadrunner symbolizing a choice of running when one doesn't fly well; and a cow skull representing death, which is a part of every life. Sandy invites you to design a few of your own quilting patterns. Besides the quilting freedom, it's your chance to use those ribbons, braids, and yarns you have been saving, but don't know why!

Number to Cut

Head — 20 black
Cape — 20 assorted fabrics
Skirt — 20 assorted fabrics

Quilt Top Assembly

1. Cut 20 blocks from peach fabric, 14½″ x 16½″. Sandy randomly placed her Indian squaw on each block to leave space for her quilting designs. If you choose to center your squaw, fold each block into quarters and finger-crease to find center. Use centering dots on skirt and cape pattern pieces for placement, and mark block.

2. Sew fringe/braid of your choice to cape and skirt of each squaw.

3. Appliqué squaw to each block in this order: skirt, head, cape.

4. For hair braids, cut 3 strands of black yarn, 13″. Tie a half-knot in the center, and braid both sides. Tie ends with contrasting yarn or ribbon. Make 20. Sew hair braid along the sides of the head with knot at the top of head.

5. Cut 25 sashing strips from black/peach print, 3″ x 16½″. Cut 24 sashing strips from black/peach print, 3″ x 14½″. Cut thirty 3″ peach accent squares.

6. Alternate 4 squaw blocks with 5 sashing strips and join, beginning with a sashing strip to form a row. Make 5 rows.

7. Alternate 4 sashing strips with 5 accent squares and join, beginning with an accent square. Make 6 sashing rows.

8. Alternate sashing rows with squaw rows and join, beginning with a sashing row.

Quilting

Outline-quilt outside the edge of the squaw appliqué. We have supplied you with a few of Sandy's quilting designs, but it is Sandy's hope that this Indian squaw will inspire you, as it did her, to design a few of your own. Randomly place quilting designs around your squaws, and quilt. Outline-quilt inside seam line of each Indian squaw block and each accent sashing block.

Finished Edges

Bind with black fabric.

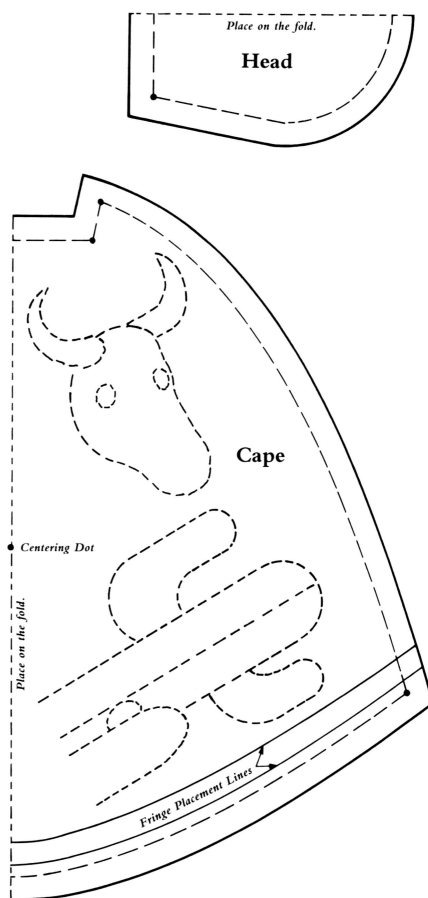

Place on the fold.

Head

Cape

Place on the fold.

● *Centering Dot*

Fringe Placement Lines

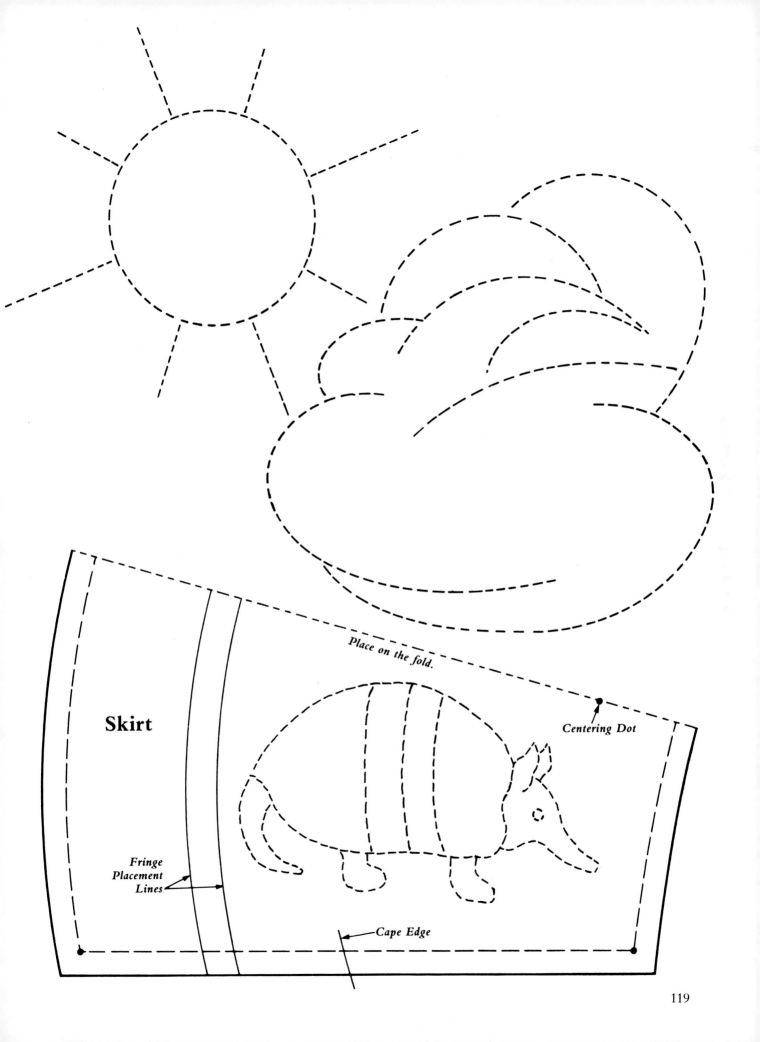

Skirt

Place on the fold.

Centering Dot

Fringe Placement Lines

Cape Edge

BEE QUILTERS

"Puttin' up a quilt" meant an excuse to visit with neighbors, close by and far away. The prospect sent waves of excitement and anticipation throughout the community.

By the 1800s the penchant for hard work had been well established as a cornerstone of the American ethic. There was no time for socializing in rural communities—there was work to be done. Homes, churches, barns, town halls, and the like were built as group projects by neighbors. So, why not a quilt, especially if it was a gift for a bride, a baby, or that lonesome bachelor down the road? Diligently, a bee of quilters would labor over framed layers of cloth to accomplish their task, but with a wink of the eye they might tell you what fun it was, too.

Today bee quilters don't need an excuse to meet. In fact, their problem may be finding a time to fit it into their busy schedules. And they do because, like their quilting ancestors, they are motivated by a love of quilting and a desire to share it with everyone.

Divine Lady of the Lake
1986

Seekers of adventure, intricate geometric configurations, harmonious color placement, and impressive craftsmanship—The Hansen Bee solidly agreed, three years ago, that the Lady of the Lake pattern would provide the excitement they craved. Store-bought fabrics in manufactured colors were for amateurs. Dyeing their own fabrics to foster a milieu of pastels was the only way to go!

Once members witnessed a morning's worth of colorfully dyed 4″ strips dancing on the clothesline, confidence expanded for the afternoon's session. "Gallon milk jugs littered the kitchen," explains Denise Sansing, the coordinator of the project, "each one containing formulas lost forever to scientific reasoning. How about some of this in there? Instinct told us there was a method to our madness." Ironed and neatly folded, the strips in their array of warm sherberty colors fascinated them, and all agreed just a little whipped cream was all that was lacking.

The grape theme with baskets was incorporated out of respect for quilting ancestors, because it was one of their favorite motifs. Padded and appliquéd grape leaves fall as if a good wind has blown them, and to show the Bee's playfulness and free spirit. For textural richness and accentuation, white baskets overflowing with grapes are sculptured, using Italian cording and trapunto techniques.

The Hansen Bee members are Denise Sansing, Fran Hansen, Barbara Jo Fish, Vivian Johnson, Maria Richardson, Jane Hinke, Mary Ruth Silhavy, Cleeta Cox, Sharon Andersen, Eilene Hamilton, Karen Jimenez, Nancy Lenz, Cheryl Olson, Donna Randolph, Cornelia Thomas, Mary Terry, Angie Stearns, and Virginia Gray.

The Hansen Bee
McAllen, Texas

Focused in their quilting endeavors, 12 women, under the umbrella of the Rio Grande Valley Quilt Guild, converged to form The Hansen Bee. As Denise Sansing explains it, "Originally, we were 12 women who enjoyed each other's company, but admittedly had very individual ideas about quilting. If there's any one reason it worked out so well, it's because we all wanted it to so much."

Members unanimously decided to name their bee in honor of Fran Hansen, 1922-1985, who so influenced and nurtured their lives. As one member expressed it, "She managed to touch innumerable lives in a positive way with her intelligence, wit, and thoughtfulness. She organized the Rio Grande Valley Quilt Guild and served as its president for the first two years."

Since 1983, the Bee has met weekly at a member's home to share quilting projects and explore new techniques collectively. These women concur in their quilting attitude. As Denise summarizes, "We all share a sense of awe concerning our quilting heritage—the social aspects, the commitment given by women coping in a time when life made a different set of demands, the innate sense of design of quiltmakers long ago that still managed to affect us so deeply, their workmanship, and the ability to foresee past their own lives to a time when something they made would live on—these things provide our inspiration."

Divine Lady of the Lake

Finished Quilt Size
90″ x 90″

Number of Blocks and Finished Size
12 Lady of the Lake
  blocks—18″ x 18″ each

Fabric Requirements
Pastels	—2 yd.
Purple	—2¾ yd.
Orange	—2½ yd.
Cream	—5 yd.
Green	—2 yd.
Backing	—5¼ yd.
Binding	—1¼ yd.

Number to Cut
Template A	—360 pastels
	360 cream
Template B	—7 green
Template C	—23 green
Template D	—16 green

Quilt Top Assembly

1. Cut 18 purple and 18 cream 12″ right triangles and add seam allowances. Join a purple 12″ triangle to a cream 12″ triangle at long edge. Join 20 cream triangles (A) to 20 pastel triangles (A) to form squares. Use cream/pastel squares to form a sawtooth border around a purple/cream square. Start by placing the tip of a pastel triangle to the tip of the purple triangle; arrange cream/pastel triangles around larger square, so that cream/pastel triangles always alternate. (Refer to color silhouette of quilt.) Make 8 blocks.

2. Make 6 half-blocks with purple 12″ triangles, and 6 half-blocks with cream 12″ triangles. Sawtooth strips are joined as before, this time using 9 squares and 2 triangles at ends. Again, begin layout with tip of pastel triangle joined to tip of purple triangle; or with tip of cream triangle joined to tip of cream triangle.

3. Prepare 4 purple 12″ triangles and 4 cream 12″ triangles for trapunto and Italian cording. Trace basket pattern on cream triangles

One-half of basket pattern for Italian cording

and grape pattern on purple triangles. Insert cording for basket pattern, and quilt along both sides of cording. Complete grape trapunto, and pin bias for basket handles in place. Be sure all 4 handles are equally placed. Appliqué and quilt outside seam line of handle. Join purple triangles to cream triangles. Complete Lady of the Lake block as above for all 4.

4. Join blocks into diagonal rows as shown in Quilt Setting Diagram below. Join rows.

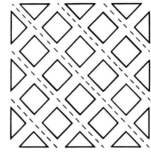

Quilt Setting Diagram

5. Cut 4 border strips, 2½″ wide, from orange; join to quilt, and miter corners.

6. Cut 4 border strips, 2½″ wide, from cream; join to quilt, and miter corners.

7. Cut 4 border strips, 3½″ wide, from purple; join to quilt, and miter corners.

Quilting and Grape Appliqué

Outline-quilt ¼″ inside seam lines of all triangles (A). Quilt grape and grape leaf patterns in cream and purple triangles. Once quilting is complete, randomly place grapevine (bias strips) over quilt. Pin bias and leaves before appliquéing, to assure a pleasing design. For dimension, The Hansen Bee padded their grape leaves before appliquéing. Appliqué leaves and vines into place. Quilt lines on grape leaves to represent leaf veins. Outline-quilt outside appliqué seam lines.

Finished Edges

Bind with cream fabric.

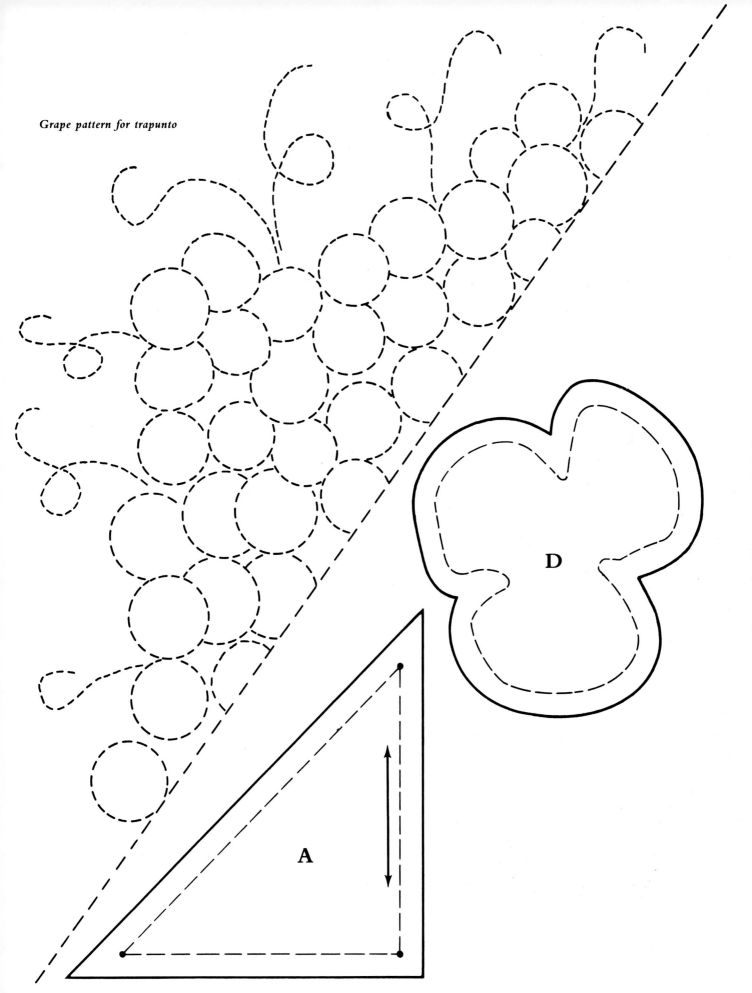

Grape pattern for trapunto

D

A

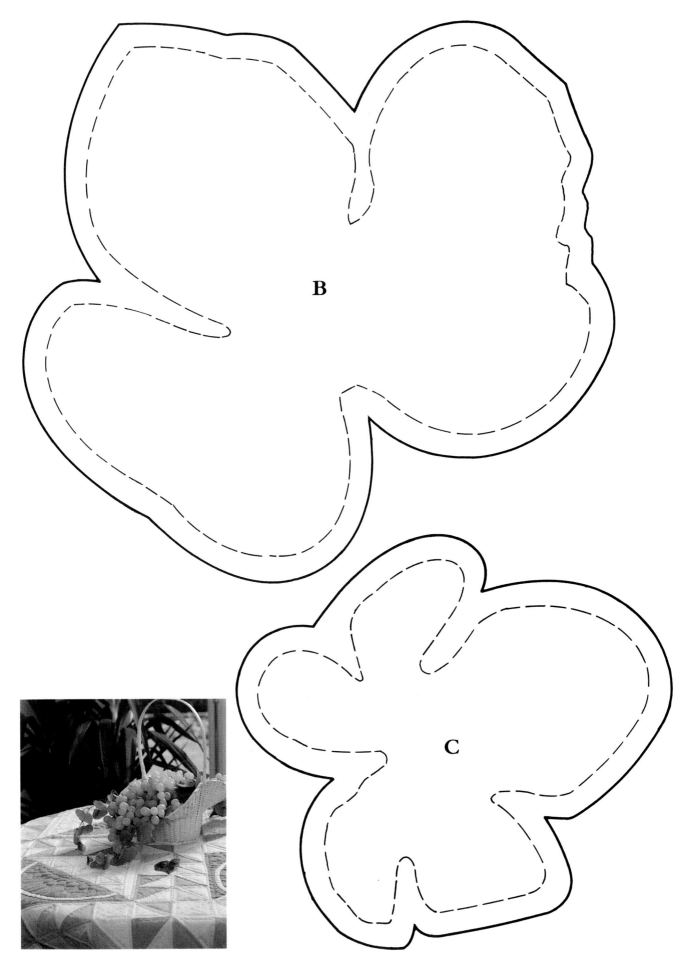

B

C

126

Mississippi Valley Quilters Guild

Davenport, Iowa

The goal of each meeting of the Mississippi Valley Quilters Guild is for it to be a learning experience. Workshops, slide presentations, and nationally known speakers and teachers are just a few of the monthly program offerings. Composed of 110 active members, the guild participates in community quilting projects. Its most recent project was a quilt donated to the Ronald McDonald House in Chicago. Outreach programs include lecturing and demonstrating quilting techniques by guild members to churches, schools, and other groups throughout the community. Guild members also conduct quilting demonstrations at a booth at the Mississippi Valley Fair each year.

Financial support comes from $12-a-year dues and a quilt raffle, held every two years. On alternate years, members donate quilted items for sale at a bazaar, held at a local shopping center, for non-profit organizations.

Hearts and Flowers
1985

Polished pink tulips, encased in silhouetted hearts, extend amid bouquets of flowers like spokes on a wheel. The soft, flowing lines of this eye-catching medallion are offset by the perpendicularity of the checkerboard squares. Quilters will appreciate the extensive quilting of feathered hearts on wide, white border strips. Members attribute part of *Hearts and Flowers'* charm to the fact that a fabric that coordinates with the rose and cream prints was available for border accents.

The twenty-five guild members who worked on *Hearts and Flowers* were Julie Klindt, Edie Borgel, Mary Jo McCabe, Bev Salmonson, Pam Duffy, Linda Haugen, Ginny Peine, Marian Behrens, Shirley DeWys, Darlene Neff, Sharon Roehlk, Mary Ann Curran, Frances Fostrom, Winnifred Petersen, Claire Schwarz, Marcia Taylor, Cheryl Bean, Lois Burke, Charlotte Grymonprez, June LeBow, Virginia King, Arlene Solomon, Joan Williams, Beulah Spaulding, Sally Frye, and Arlene Shindelar.

Hearts and Flowers

Finished Quilt Size
96″ x 112″

Number of Blocks and Finished Size
28 checkerboard
  blocks—4½″ x 4½″ each
80 checkerboard
  blocks—7½″ x 7½″ each

Fabric Requirements
Rose print for
  checkerboard   — 2¾ yd.
Rose print
  for appliqué   — ¼ yd.
Green print   — 1¼ yd.
Blue print   — ½ yd.
Maroon   — ½ yd.
White print   — 9¾ yd.
Rose print with
  stripe for borders— 6 yd.
Maroon for binding— 1¼ yd.
White print
  for backing   — 10 yd.

Number to Cut
Template A   — 360 rose print
                 for checkerboard
                 360 white print
Template B   — 126 rose print
                 for checkerboard
                 126 white print
Template C   — 1 rose print
                 for appliqué
Template D   — 1 maroon
Template E   — 4 rose print
                 for appliqué
Template F   — 4 maroon
Template G   — 4 rose print
                 for appliqué
Template H   — 4 green print
Template I   — 8 green print
Template J   — 4 green print
Template K   — 4 maroon
Template L   — 8 maroon
Template M   — 1 maroon
Template N   — 8 blue print
Template O   — 4 blue print
Template P   — 4 blue print

Quilt Top Assembly
1. Cut 24½″ square from white print. Appliqué hearts and flowers to square. The Mississippi Valley Quilters chose to machine-appliqué their pieces.
2. Cut 4 lengths of striped fabric, 2″ x 27½″, join to square, and miter corners.
3. Make 14 checkerboard blocks, using 5 rose print 2″ squares and 4 white print 2″ squares. Make 14 checkerboard blocks, using 4 rose print 2″ squares and 5 white print 2″ squares. Alternate 8 checkerboard blocks to form checkerboard row. Make 2 rows. Make 2 more rows, alternating 6 checkerboard blocks. Join to appliquéd medallion.
4. Cut 4 lengths of striped fabric, 1¼″ x 37¾″, join to quilt, and miter corners.
5. Cut 2 lengths of white print, 7½″ x 68″, and 2 lengths, 15½″ x 38″. Join the 38″ pieces to top and bottom of quilt square. Join the 68″ pieces to opposite sides.
6. Cut 2 lengths of striped fabric, 1¼″ x 53½″, and 2 lengths, 1¼″ x 69½″. Join to quilt, and miter the corners.
7. Make 40 checkerboard blocks, using 5 rose print 3″ squares and 4 white print 3″ squares. Make 40 checkerboard blocks, using 4 rose print 3″ squares and 5 white print 3″ squares. Join 2 checkerboard blocks to make a small checkerboard row for quilt sides. Make 18 rows. Join 9 rows lengthwise to form a column. Make 2 columns. Join columns to quilt sides. Alternate 11 blocks to make a checkerboard row. Make 4 rows. Join 2 rows lengthwise for top of quilt, and 2 rows for bottom of quilt.
8. Cut 4 lengths of striped fabric, 1¼″ wide, join to quilt, and miter corners.
9. Cut 4 lengths of white print, 3¾″ wide, join to quilt, and miter corners.
10. Cut 4 lengths of striped fabric, 2″ wide, join to quilt, and miter corners.

Quilting
Outline-quilt ¼″ outside appliqué edge, and inside seam line of center square. Outline-quilt ¼″ inside seam lines of all white print squares. Outline-quilt ¼″ inside seam lines of all striped borders. Quilt 3 feathered heart patterns in large white print sections. Quilt 5″ scallops along last white print border strip.

Finished Edges
Bind with maroon fabric.

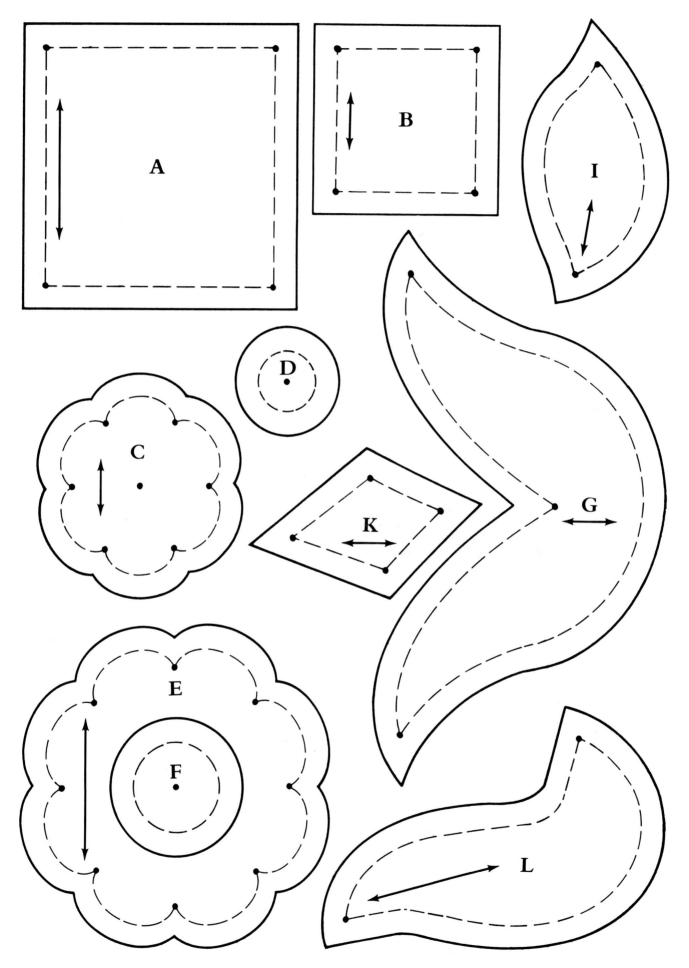

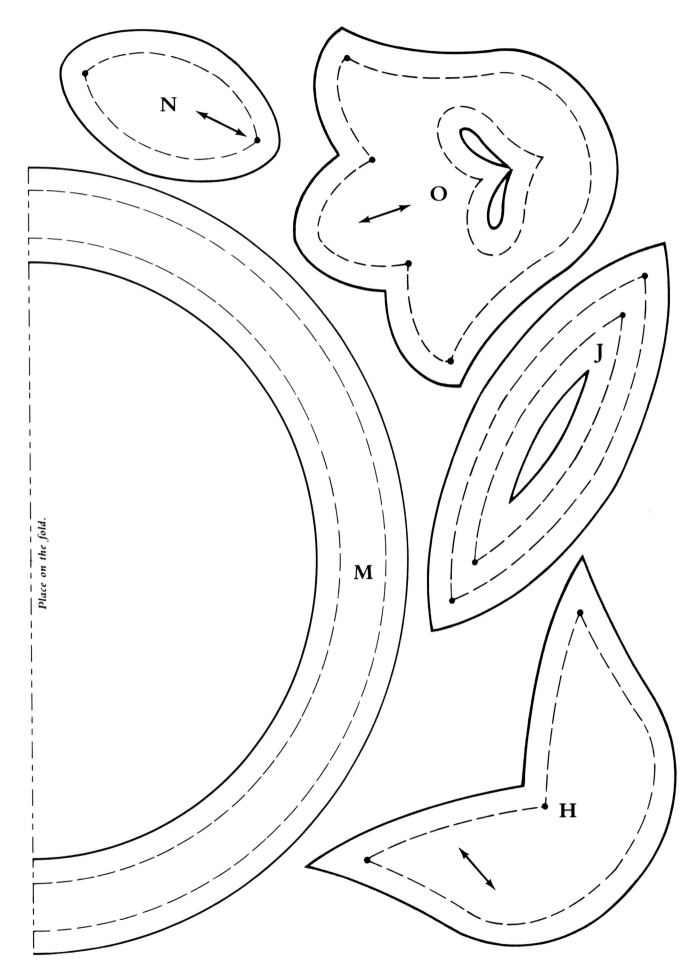

N

O

J

M

H

Place on the fold.

130

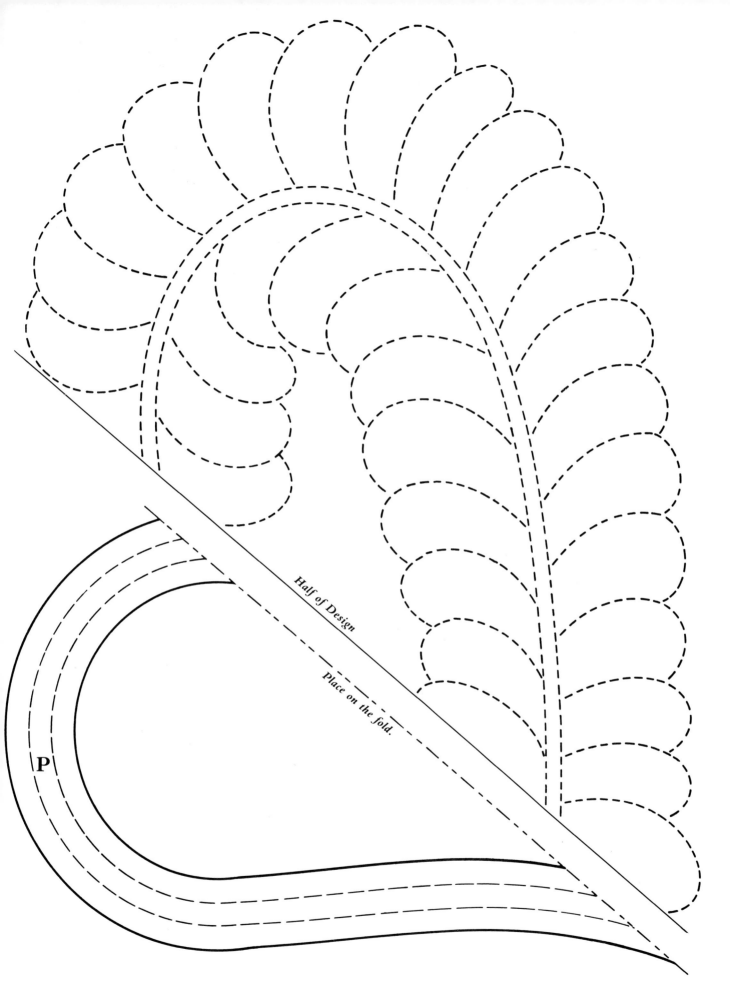

Half of Design

Place on the fold.

P

Krazy Quilter's Club

Temple Terrace, Florida

Krazy Quilter's Club members (left to right)— Mary Caltagirone, Matilda Pelaez, Marie Fischer (standing), Eva Knoten, and Blanche Young—are busy working on another beautiful quilt.

Just "krazy" about quilting is the unified cry of these ladies. These 35 quilters live up to their name, with the happiness they share in quilting together and the quilts they have made.

Their founder, Sadie Bell, wanted everyone in the world exposed to quilting. In 1977 she organized a group of interested stitchers to meet in her home. Shortly thereafter the membership increased, and meetings were moved to the local recreation center. At that time, it was decided that there would be no dues, because Sadie felt this might keep some ladies away. Instead, the hat was and still is passed at every meeting, and members contribute whatever they wish (usually a quarter each week). Whatever money is collected is used to purchase fabric and other items necessary to make the next quilt. The club meets every Tuesday at a member's home, except during Christmas holidays, so it doesn't take long to accumulate money for the next quilt project.

They prefer to lap-quilt, and usually five to eight ladies work on one quilt. Upon completion, a drawing is held. Those who worked on the quilt from start to finish are eligible to win that quilt. A member can only win once, and must work on two complete quilts after joining the club, to qualify. The winner is then in charge of organizing the next project, under the supervision of the president. As President Marie Fischer says, "This is another way we use to teach more about quilting. You know, if you are in charge, you learn more—right?!"

Rose Spray
1985

The stitches of the talented hands of Eva Knoten, Marie M. Fischer, Mary Caltagirone, Blanche Young, Dixie Pereira-Muzzi, Matilda Pelaez, Jean Johnston, and Nancy Waters merged as the stitches of one to form this elegant floral quilt. Softly portrayed in peaches and creams, *Rose Spray* is a traditional pattern, appliquéd on a large square and then lap-quilted. Each rosebud is embroidered with wisps of forest green accents. Wide borders are the trellis for climbing roses to envelop the symmetrical rose spray blocks.

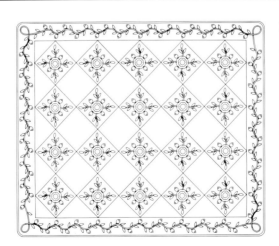

Rose Spray

Finished Quilt Size
87″ x 106″

Number of Blocks and Finished Size
20 appliquéd blocks—13″ x 13″ each
12 quilted blocks—13″ x 13″ each

Fabric Requirements
Peach print   — ¾ yd.
Cream/peach print — ¼ yd.
Peach   — ¼ yd.
Off-white   —7½ yd.

Cream/peach print
  for backing — 10¾ yd.
  (based on 44″ fabric)
Forest green for stems,
  leaves, buds, and
  ¼″ bias binding — 4 yd.

Embroidery Floss
4 skeins leaf green

Number to Cut
Template A — 80 solid green
Template B — 154 solid green
Template C — 154 solid green
Template D — 152 solid green

Template E — 20 solid peach
Template F — 20 cream/peach
                print
Template G — 152 peach print
Template H — 20 peach print

Quilt Top Assembly
1. Cut 32 blocks, 13½″ square,
from off-white fabric. Fold into
quarters, and finger-crease to find
center. Mark for quilting and/or appliqué. Appliqué 20 blocks in rose
spray pattern. Embroider bud areas,
using 2 strands of leaf green thread
(see Embroidery Diagram).

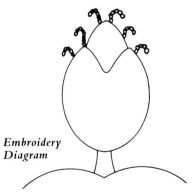

Embroidery Diagram

2. Prepare all 32 blocks for lap quilting. Quilt ⅛″ outside appliqué edge. Quilt the remaining 12 blocks in the rose wreath pattern.

3. Cut 4 right triangles for corners, so that finished triangle sides equal 9¼″ each and the hypotenuse equals 13⅛″. Cut 14 right triangles for sides of quilt, so that finished triangle sides equal 13″ each and the hypotenuse equals 18½″. Prepare corner and side triangles for lap quilting. Quilt one-fourth of the rose wreath pattern (1 flower) on corner triangles, and one-half of the rose wreath pattern (4 flowers) on each side triangle.

4. Set blocks diagonally into rows, alternating appliquéd/quilted blocks with quilted blocks, as shown on Quilt Setting Diagram. Join side and corner triangles to complete rows. Join rows. Quilt ¼″ from seam lines of each block.

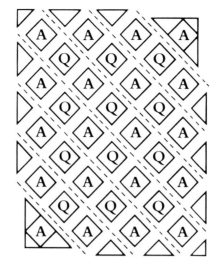

Quilt Setting Diagram

5. Cut 4 border strips, 8½″ wide. Mark for appliquéd rose vine pattern, except for 8″ to 10″ of the corner areas. Leave this free so that corners may be mitered. Appliqué

border strips. Join border strips to quilt, and miter corners. Complete appliquéd design with rose vine loop on the corners. Embroider bud areas.

6. Prepare border strips for quilting, and quilt ⅛″ outside appliqué.

Finished Edges
Round corners, and bind with forest green.

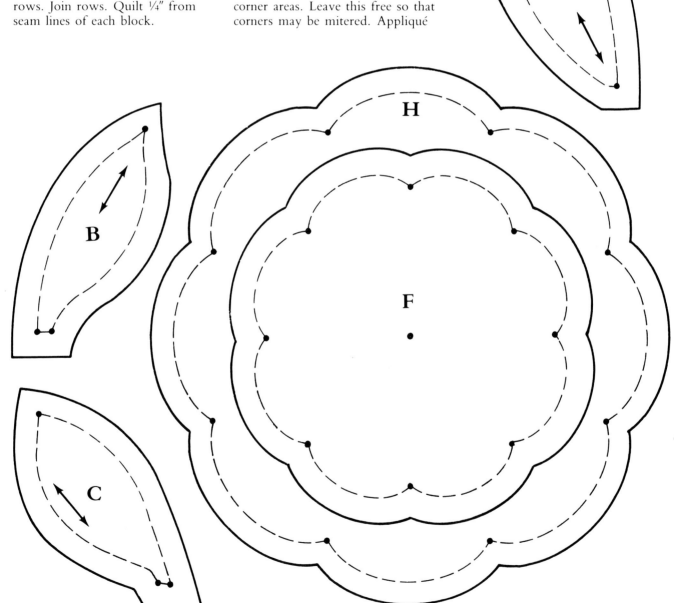

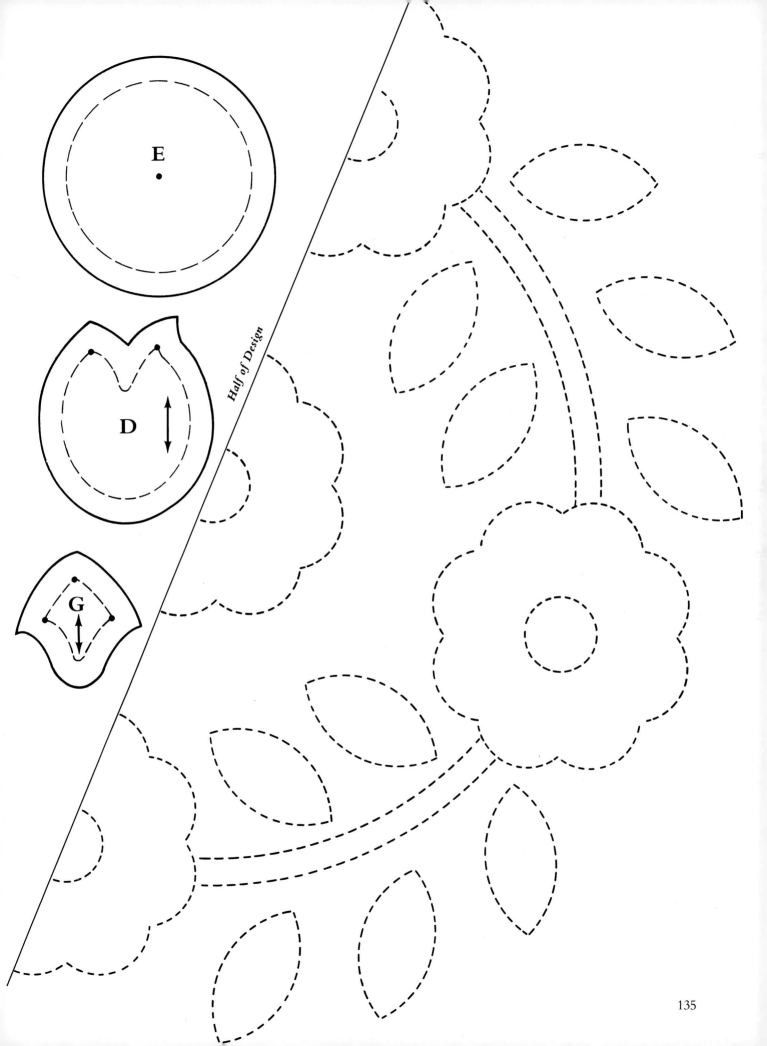

E

D

G

Half of Design

DESIGNER GALLERY

Until the advent of industrialized society, quilt-making was not considered an art form. It was simply a matter of necessity, of keeping warm. Not until quilts were unnecessary could they be used as art. "Designer Gallery" is not just a collection of quilted works of art, but a collection of inspirations. These are quilts that we hope will encourage you to experiment and attempt that which you had only dreamed heretofore. They are visions by dedicated quiltmakers of the heights that quilting can reach. These patchwork artisans are our quilting pioneers.

Marcia Karlin

Highland Park, Illinois

In the last two years, Marcia Karlin has explored the parameters of quiltmaking, both in color and fabric selection as well as overall design. She isn't afraid to try new things, and is presently involved in fabric painting. She sells many of her quilts, but admits, like most quilters, that her primary motivation is personal satisfaction. She notes, though, "The knowledge that others appreciate my work enough to pay for acquiring a piece reinforces my belief that I have found a worthwhile vocation." Read more about Marcia and see her dazzling Log Cabin wall hanging, *Metamorphosis*, in "Log Cabin Turnaround."

Palma Sola Sunrise
1985
Squares and triangles of pinks, greens, blues, and yellows are united to abstractly emulate the sand, water, palms, sailboats, stucco buildings, and sky of a typical Florida landscape. The mirror-image block pattern reflects printed images, just as a shimmering lake tosses its images to shore.

Nightfall
1986
Japanese yukata prints, chintzes, and cotton blends produce this prismatic array of color. What began as a study of isometric triangles became a fascination with the spatial illusions caused by contrasting fabrics. As Marcia pieced a progression of light to dark triangles across her quilt, the name for this quilt became apparent to her.

Sue Franklin

Wimberley, Texas

This home economics major has been quilting for 30 years and has been a professional fiber artist for most of them. She combines quilting with her batik, silk screen, or appliqué work, and applauds the dimensional aspect it adds to her wall hangings. All her designs are originals, and she is adept at mixing just the right amount of hand quilting with machine quilting to provide definition, as well as textural richness, to many of her works.

Sue is a member of the Contemporary Fiber Designers of San Antonio. Her works have won many awards and have been exhibited in museums and shows throughout Texas.

Down at the Bay
1976

Stained-glass imagery is used to create this tranquil harbor scene of moored sailboats. Couched strands of bulky yarns of black, blue, and purple cast rippling shadows upon the shimmering water's surface. Juxtaposed patches of corals and blues simulate a broken-cloud horizon. Machine quilting and hand stitchery are combined to form the ship masts. Sue made this large wall hanging shortly after her family had sold their bay house. It expresses her love and longing for the coastal region and the sea. "This quilt is a very personal one," says Sue.

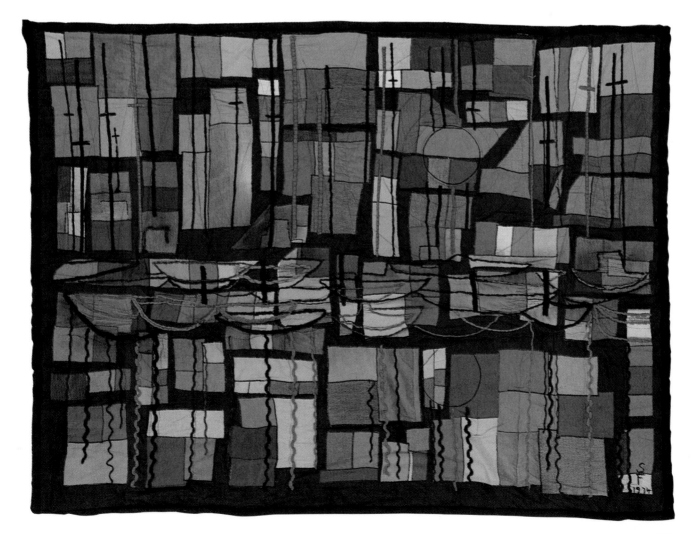

JoAnn Brandt

Dinuba, California

"I just love to do quilting. 'Nothing could be finer than to quilt in my recliner in the evening,' " sings JoAnn. This self-taught quilter is hooked on quilting. She says, "You hear about quilters doing silly things such as driving great distances to a quilt show, sniffing out a fabric store miles upwind, callused fingers, and the like. Well, it's all true! Just ask my husband and kids."

About ten years ago JoAnn attended a Mennonite Relief Sale, and the quilts really appealed to her. She gave quilting a try, and for the past nine years has made and donated a quilt to the Relief Sale. She also spends one morning a week quilting with several other ladies for the Relief Sale. When asked where she gets her inspiration, she replied, "I thought you knew what quilters do at night when they can't sleep."

Flower Box
1986

This elegant white-on-white quilt is the first quilt JoAnn has made for herself. "I designed it with lots of quilting *for me!*" exclaims JoAnn. "I've made and worked on so many quilts for others, I figured it was time I made one for me." Approximately 1,100 yards of quilting thread perforate the ocean of white to dimensionalize JoAnn's flower boxes. JoAnn used a size 12 needle when quilting her ¼" cross-hatching. "I wanted something that showed off my quilting," brags JoAnn. And she adds, "I hope it's less than ten years before I make time to make another quilt for me."

Stephanie Santmyers

Greensboro, North Carolina

Stephanie, a quilter for four years, has yet to make a traditional block. "I enjoy looking at traditional quilts but haven't the desire to make one," says Stephanie. Trained as an artist and presently an assistant professor of art at North Carolina A & T State University, Stephanie became a self-taught quilter because of a need for a bed quilt. Now, quilting is one of the mediums she displays in the competitions required to maintain her position as art professor.

Stephanie calls quilt designing her dream time, when ideas fill many sheets of paper. She plays pattern games with pieces of plain white paper, cutting them into different shapes and sizes, sometimes using mirrors to see what effect repeated shapes would have. Once she is satisfied, the design is glued to a larger sheet of paper and painted with tempera paint. Often Stephanie will sort through her fabrics and let them give her ideas.

"My involvement is complete," confesses Stephanie. "The project is my first and last thought every day."

When Comets Collide
1986

Dynamic explosions of reds, blues, and yellows in fabrics and ribbons mesh to present this kaleidoscope of color. Colorful scientific photos of the core of Halley's comet inspired Stephanie to create this gem. "I remember anticipating Halley's comet many years ago," says Stephanie. "It has been a disappointment to me because it's so tiny. This quilt is my attempt to find excitement with the idea of comets."

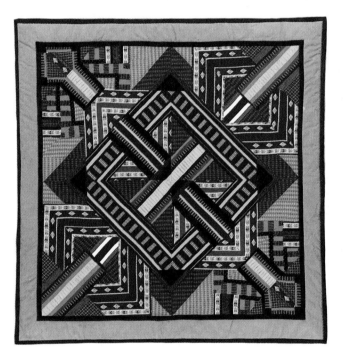

Mixed Signals
1986

Calm quiet colors counterbalance this powerful display of geometric shapes. Patterned beams of yellow, gold, and red, like steel girders, crisscross and connect complementary squares. Pleated fabric and corduroy are used to make the surface similar to a relief. Stephanie admits, "The title of this quilt reflects what it was like to make."

Charlotte Warr Andersen

Kearns, Utah

This accomplished quilter makes a variety of quilt types but prefers pieced quilts. "I enjoy the actual construction of the quilt top, because that is where the design emanates from and is the heart of the quilt," says Charlotte. Charlotte considers herself a professional, and can be found quilting some twenty to forty hours a week in her living room, to be with her family. "My quilting gives me much pleasure," says Charlotte.

Read more about Charlotte in "Quilts Across America" and enjoy her majestic *Seven Sisters Medallion* quilt.

Upstream
1984

Charlotte made this quilt for her brother, a dentist and avid sport fisherman, and, as Charlotte describes him, "an all-around nice guy." Designing this wall hanging for him was Charlotte's way of repaying him for all the free dentistry. She varied the traditional pattern, Delectable Mountains, and corner-mounted pieced pine trees to portray the outdoors that her brother loves so much. *Upstream* is the compilation of at least 20 to 30 different fabrics 'ranging from printed cottons to glimmering silks. It won Best of Show at the Springville Art Museum Quilt Exhibit 1984, Springville, Utah. "I am very pleased with the way this quilt turned out," remarks Charlotte. "There is a lot to look at in it."

142

Resources

Many of our quilters gained inspiration for their quilt designs from previously published designs and patterns. Below is a list of those publications.

1. Patti Connor's *The Big Black Quilt* — Hopkins, Mary Ellen: *The It's Okay If You Sit On My Quilt Book,* p. 61. Atlanta, Georgia: Yours Truly, Inc., 1982.
2. Bobbie Fuhrmann's *Queen's Petticoat* — "Quilt-as-you-go Queen's Petticoat." In *Needlecraft for Today,* edited by Fredrica Daugherty, pp. 13 and 27. Ft. Worth, Texas: Happy Hands Publishing Co., (May/June) 1979. *Queen's Petticoat* also appears in *Quilts from Happy Hands.* Ft. Worth, Texas: Happy Hands Publishing Co., 1981.

3. Nancy Henebry's *As I Wait* — The pomegranate pattern is from *Mountain Mist Catalog of Classic Quilt Patterns,* p. 19. The Stearns Technical Textiles Company, 100 Williams Street, Cincinnati, Ohio.
4. Martha Street's *Baltimore Wreath* — "Appliqué for the Holidays—Baltimore Wreath and Meadow Wreath, and Easy Quiltmaking Lesson No. 11." In *Quilter's Newsletter Magazine,* edited by Bonnie Leman, pp. 10-11 and 32. Wheatridge, Colorado: Leman Publications, Inc., (Nov/Dec) 1981.

Special thanks to **Parisian, Inc.,** Riverchase Galleria, of Birmingham, Alabama, for sharing their clothing to coordinate with Christine Hile's coat and jacket.